MODERN JUDO

TECHNIQUES OF EAST AND WEST

PETER SEISENBACHER & GEORGE KERR

The Crowood Press

First published in 1991 by
The Crowood Press Ltd
Ramsbury, Marlborough
Wiltshire SN8 2HR

Paperback edition 1997

British Library Cataloguing in Publication Data

A catalogue record for this book is available from the British Library.

ISBN 1 86126 020 2

Acknowledgements
This book would not have been possible without Eddie Ferrie who helped to write it. He spent many hours with both of us and put the project together. Similarly, we are grateful, as so many Judoka have been before us, for the expertise of judo photographer David Finch, both for the session photographs and the access to his competition portfolio. Our thanks also go to John O'Brien and the High Wycombe Judo Centre where the demonstration pictures were taken, and to Paul Ajala and Nicolas Soames who were alert throwing partners.

Note Throughout this book, the pronouns 'he', 'him' and 'his' are intended to apply to both men and women. It is important in sport, as elsewhere, that men and women have equal status and opportunities.

Photographs by David Finch

Typeset by Inforum, Portsmouth
Printed and bound in Great Britain

Contents

Preface

It was a happy combination of circumstances that brought Peter Seisenbacher and myself together. I had gone from being a competitor and a club instructor to occupy a position as a Class One international referee but after the 1976 Montreal Olympics had decided to resign from refereeing over a difference of opinion regarding the interpretation of newly introduced passivity rulings intended to penalize the adoption of excessively defensive postures in contest. I had just seen the Austrian heavyweight lose to Keith Remfry and had said to Kurt Kucera, the President of the Austrian Federation, that if I had been coaching the Austrian team they could have won two medals. I did not apply for the position of Team Manager to the British Team, which was vacated by Ray Ross, because it required a full-time commitment and I had a business to run. It was taken over by Dave Starbrook and Tony Macconnell.

Britain's loss was to be Austria's gain, because Kucera took me at my word and, on the recommendation of Lutz Liscka, the Austrian team trainer, a journalist who had come fifth in the Munich Olympics and had spent some time training with me at the Renshuden in 1962, I was offered a part-time appointment to begin coaching the Austrian squad.

My first impressions of Peter Seisenbacher were not especially memorable. He was a tall, skinny, lanky brown belt who stood out from the rest only in that he was a bit more determined and was already quite good at *newaza*. Liscka had been especially keen to get me enlisted in the running of the team because he had problems with some of the more extrovert members of the squad like Klaus Wallas and Jurek Jatowtt, but discipline was never a problem once I was in charge; I put the responsibility for their performances in their own hands.

Taking on the Austrian team at this time was quite an interesting proposition and our first outing involved going to Paris for training and a team match with the French. I met Jean Paul Coche, ex-European Champion and one of the French coaches there and, when I told him of my new job, he quipped, 'You are starting out as a team manager in the best possible place: at the bottom!' Despite the obvious humour in his words, there was a ring of truth to them. We lost 9–0 with Peter Koestenburger managing to draw. However, Koestenburger was young, aggressive, strong and full of potential and in the Junior World Championships, with my coaching later that year in Barcelona, he had just had the edge he needed to win the junior world title. Success breeds success and, once his team mates saw that one of their group could do it, they redoubled their efforts to match his success.

Seisenbacher's breakthrough came in the Junior European Championships in 1979 when he won a bronze medal. In the same year, in the Senior Europeans, aged twenty, he got to the final, coming from behind to throw Peter Donnelly of Great Britain for ippon with his *ouchi-gari*. He was beaten in the final by Iaskevitch, but he had had a tantalizing taste of what success might be like and he was hungry for more. After a disappointing performance in the 1980 Olympics, Seisenbacher decided he needed to be trained in Japan. I spent ten days there setting things up for him and he went out there initially for two six-week periods per year. Robert van de Walle used the same system as preparation for major championships because, like Seisenbacher, he

Fig 1 George Kerr (right) with Tony Macconnell and one of the great European judoka, 1981 world champion, Neil Adams, at the 1982 European Championships in Rostock.

could not get enough strong training partners at home.

The great advantage of being based in Austria, though, was that it is situated in the heart of Europe, where East meets West and access to hard competitions is virtually unlimited. Competitions like the Hungary Cup, the Bulgarian Open, Potsdam, the Czech Open, the Tournoi de Paris and the East and West German Opens were easily reached and provided perfect tune-up events to hone the skills that were trained in practice to perfection. This central geographic location was the main reason that Professor Shigeyoshi Matsumae built the International Budo Centre there.

The other big advantage that Seisenbacher had over many western judoka was that he was a soldier. In Austria, national service is compulsory, lasting nine months, but any young, budding judo man who wants to try can go off to thesaurus school (the Sudstatt) and do full-time judo. Accommodation is arranged and they can earn 10,000 schillings per month and receive full board. If they achieve a medal in a Class B tournament, they are permitted to carry on.

Seisenbacher thrived on hard training and particularly on the Japanese approach. As his judo got better and I helped prepare the way for him, he began to realize the value of a coach in a way he had not before. After deciding to make a three-month visit to Japan in 1981, he came back to Austria in March a changed fighter. Japan had transformed him; he never thought in materialistic terms, just of judo. He realized my value to him as a coach who understood the Japanese mind and the system: *budoshi*, the way of judo. Sadly this no longer seems to exist. But we spent much of the time at Tokai University, run by Nobuyuki Sato, who had himself twice won world titles and the coveted All-Japan Championships. Nobuyuki Sato is one of the few *sensei* in Japan who still tries to instil *budoshi* into his students. Since, in general, the sporting ethos of the West had replaced the traditional Japanese way. Most no longer regard their training as training for life. Sato still preserves the traditional New Year's Eve training: practising judo from 11.00 p.m. – 1.00 a.m.; then sweeping out the dojo afterwards prior to a celebratory meal in preparation for the New Year.

From 1982, it was purely a matter of time before Seisenbacher achieved the success he deserved and, despite a disappointing World Championships in 1983, the prospect of the gold medal in Los Angeles grew ever more possible. In Homer's epic poem, *The Iliad*, the greatest warriors were always rewarded by the gods for their courage by an *aristeia*, a time when they could not be beaten by their opponents and glory would be theirs. For Peter Seisenbacher, that time was due in 1984.

The same determination and confidence that won him his gold medal in the 1984 Los Angeles Olympics took him on to win the World Championships in 1985, the European Championships in 1986 and, most remarkably, a second Olympic gold medal in the 1988 Games in Seoul, South Korea – something no other judo man had ever achieved. The approach that had allowed him to achieve this was a modern one. As Seisenbacher's coach, I was mother, father and trainer all rolled into one. I did things for him

that the traditional Japanese *sensei* would have considered unthinkable. The Japanese way has always been unquestioning obedience, while in the West the approach is more lively; values shift and progress is made through dialogue. To a certain extent, we were combining both approaches to get the best out of each and the balance was quite delicate.

The most telling example of the difference became the subject of a huge article in an Austrian newspaper and was based on a minute and apparently trivial comment. When we were in Japan, prior to the 1988 Olympics, I used to get up in the morning and make breakfast for Seisenbacher. On one particular day, when he was feeling stiff and sore, slightly overweight from eating too many Big Macs with chips and milk shakes at Tokyo Macdonalds, bored by the innumerable dojo training sessions and disgruntled by the prospect of another hard day he said to me, 'George, there is too much butter on my toast'. The complaint was like a slap in the face to someone who was himself a 7th dan, one of the highest of western grades and the product of the traditional Japanese system, and I had to ask myself, 'What am I doing here with this young guy?' It was the beginning of a dialogue, one of many, that helped us to understand exactly what we were doing and what we were out to achieve. The result is history.

This book sets out that history and highlights the collaborative, analytical approach to judo that really made the difference to Peter Seisenbacher's career and which has to be the basis for the development of our modern judo, a judo effective enough to win two Olympic gold medals, yet a judo that goes beyond mere sport.

1 The Japanese Tradition:
A Personal History by George Kerr

BEGINNINGS

Judo has always been for me a combat sport, first and foremost. I grew up in Edinburgh in Scotland in the 1940s and 50s in a social environment where physical toughness was prized and fighting and physical competition were ever present elements. Combat sports were in my blood and had been causing trouble in my family even before I was born. My father had been a prize fighter going around the boxing booths and making a living taking on all comers, although in fact he had no need to, being the son of well-to-do parents who owned a haulage firm. His parents strongly disapproved of his activities and, as a result, there was a rift in their relationship for some time. When he met the woman who was to be my mother, my father had to give up boxing before she would agree to marry him and he subsequently became a bus-driver.

As a consequence of my father's passion for boxing, I was to grow up in a tough, working-class world rather than a comfortable middle-class environment. Many people, who are privileged to grow up in this latter environment might sigh or even pity such circumstances, but I am a great believer in the old saying, 'It's an ill wind that blows nobody any good'. Looking back, I do not regret the start I had in life one bit because in the end your life is what you make it, and that is a lesson I learned from judo.

Despite being unable to take part in boxing, because of his promise to my mother, my father remained a keen fan, and one of the earliest memories I have is of him waking me up at 3.30 a.m. to listen to a Joe Louis fight on the radio. Naturally, as a young and impressionable child, I shared my father's enthusiasm for the noble art and was keen to follow in his footsteps. However, my first experiences of combat sports were anything but encouraging.

As a fairly small thirteen year old, I ventured down to the Leith Victoria boxing club where I began training under the auspices of Mr Tommy Lee. Being a short aggressive type of fighter, I quickly found myself in the ring with taller and often heavier boys. The glamour of boxing faded rapidly as I repeatedly found myself being thumped in the face by leather-gloved fists that seemed to come from nowhere. I was well overmatched and soon began to skip the training sessions. Boxing seemed too much the domain of the masochist for my personal tastes. However, some months later I was to discover the sport that would dominate and totally transform my life: judo.

It was a friend of my father's who introduced me to judo, a bus-driver called Eddie Stirling. He took me for the first time to the Edinburgh Judo Academy. The teacher was a man called Stan Mayo, who was reputed to be a black belt, although he was actually a green belt. Grade aside, I marvelled at his ability and the ease with which he could throw everyone else in the club around the mat. With the benefit of hindsight, I can see that he was more of a wrestler than a classical judo man, but I suppose he was my first judo hero.

I soon discovered that there was more to judo than what went on within the four walls of the Edinburgh Judo Academy when there was a club visit one evening from a rival club called Tora Scotia, or Tigers of Scotland, as they were known. Their blue belts appeared devastatingly good at judo and very sincere in their attitudes and the way that they practised and I was so deeply impressed that I asked them if I could go and practise at their club. They were based in the port of Leith, the toughest part of the city. The modern purpose-built environment that today's judo players increasingly enjoy have nothing in common with the old Tora Scotia. Judo there was judo in the raw and the facilities could not have been more primitive. The club was an old-age pensioners' hall and had no tatami, instead old bed mattresses were laid across the floor and kept in place by tying them with cords to the wall-mounted radiators that kept the old folk warm on those nights when there was no judo. The mat had to be laid for every practice and picked up afterwards.

Even getting a judogi, the sort of thing so taken for granted today, was a complicated undertaking. In my case, my mother provided the solution by purchasing a canvas sleeping bag and hand sewing a jacket and a pair of trousers out of it. My career in judo certainly could not have continued had it not been for her forbearance and willingness to effect repairs whenever necessary, which turned out to be quite frequent.

One of the most memorable moments in those early days was the visit of Ted Roakly, Scotland's first black belt, a Royal Marine Commando who was to found the Clarakwai in Kilmarnock, building the premises there and organizing promotion examinations or gradings.

By the age of thirteen, judo had become more than just a hobby for me, I lived and breathed it, I used to go straight to the Tora Scotia after school and put down the mats, generally arriving before everyone else. It became customary for me to put the gas on to make the tea for the senior players who would turn up later on, after their day's work, and have a cup before going on to practice. This became the routine every Tuesday, Thursday and Friday, with me having to rush home after practice in order to get in the house for 9.00 p.m. to avoid trouble with my parents.

Eventually I became a sort of mascot for the club and it became normal for the older members of the club to sneak me into the pub with them when they went for a drink after practising on Friday nights, although they always ensured that I only drank orange juice. One of the great strengths of the club was that it had a family atmosphere and however hard the training or practive might become, people there always cared and always retained their respect for each other. It is something I feel, looking back more than forty years, is of crucial importance in order for any club to thrive.

Steps Along the Way

At my first grading, I won my yellow belt and was thrilled by the sense of achievement and progress that this represented for me at that age. As the years pass and we reach higher grades, it becomes very easy to be blasé about grade. Personally, I regard 3rd dan to 5th dan as being the really significant grades; anyone achieving that sort of level has demonstrated that they have real ability in judo. Nevertheless, the importance of grading to children and the attendant improvement in self-image, and indeed self-esteem, ought not to be underestimated. The grading involved making a three-hour trip to Kilmarnock to be graded by John Sneath and George Macbeth and was a real adventure for a thirteen year old, I went on to get my blue belt and was graded by no less august a personage than Gunji Koizumi, 'the father of European judo', and then went on to become the youngest black belt in Scotland, by winning the grade of 1st dan in Glasgow at the age of sixteen.

One of the most memorable moments in my early judo career came in 1955 when I was

Fig 2   Judo before the era of the automatic washing machine: a judo course in St Andrews taken by Teizo Kawamura, front row, centre. A youthful George Kerr sits on his left. Kawamura was the instructor at the Budokwai from 1953–1955.

on holiday in London and practising at The Budokwai: I came across one of the best judo men of his day, Geoff Gleeson, who had just come back from Japan with his 4th dan. My first meeting with the man who was then my hero was nothing if not eventful; he threw me from pillar to post and there was almost an all out fight as a result of my youthful exuberance and fiery temper. I was probably only saved from serious physical harm for my lack of respect and control by the timely intervention of Tom McDermott, an extremely tough Glaswegian and the first Scot to represent Great Britain at judo. He was not impressed by the treatment his young fellow countryman was receiving at the hands of the English.

I remember how McDermott piped up, 'If you want to pick on anyone, pick on me!' Eventually order was restored and I apologized for my outburst. I still felt it had not been entirely unprovoked and proceeded to practise with Mr Gleeson again, acquitting myself a lot better the second time, and at least earning his respect, although he was, of course, much my superior and too experienced for me. However, he remembered me and when I later came back from Japan to win my place in the British team he was the team manager. Luckily he had a sense of humour and sufficient magnanimity for there to be no hard feelings and we always got along extremely well.

One of the most far-reaching influences on

my judo and my personality was Mr Trevor Leggett, a man to whom many of the judo men of my generation owe an enormous respect and a considerable debt. If Gunji Koizumi was the founder of judo in Great Britain, Mr Leggett was its consolidator. He saw something in me at an early age which he must have regarded as worthy of cultivation. He arranged for The Budokwai to pay half the cost of my train fare to London once every six weeks in order that I could train and learn more about judo and indeed about life.

I remember those occasions, taking the overnight train and getting into King's Cross, bleary eyed, at 6.15 a.m., and then the trek across London for training. After the training, My Leggett would take me to the theatre or the opera, then we would go out to dine and, inevitably, I would be given lists of books to read on my return to Edinburgh. In effect, I was given an education by the great man of British judo, as were so many others. He gave depth to our judo training and breadth to our social education. I count myself lucky to have been among the fortunate ones that he took under his wing. He raised my awareness in many areas, for the depth of his understanding of many complex issues was well beyond most peoples' ability to grasp at the time. For instance, he had opposed the institution of individual championships for quite a long time because of the inherently selfish nature of the competitive ethos. He insisted that judo should be a vehicle for self-improvement, not the self-aggrandizement of athletic competition. Judo was about improving the mind and the body. In the early 1950s, twelve million people practised that kind of judo in Japan alone but, by 1982 the number had dropped to four million, and this was largely because of the shift in emphasis to the sport ethic so applauded by the West.

In 1957, aged eighteen, I made it into the British team for the European Championships, but was dropped in favour of the much more experienced and brilliant judo man, Mr John Newman, and Britain won without my efforts. I decided, after taking advice from many of the top figures in judo at the time, that what I needed to do to improve and maximize my potential was to go to Japan. Indeed my education would not have been complete without doing so. However, in the 1950s it was somewhat more problematic to travel to the Far East than it is today.

I worked as an engineer for a while to earn the money to pay my fare, and I left England on the 24 December 1957, aged eighteen. The fare that Christmas Eve was £99 and the journey took over a month, travelling by train and

Fig 3   A more scrubbed version of Kerr and Kawamura in the same year.

Fig 4   A club randori in 1954 – before George Kerr left for Japan. Here, he is throwing right-handed. Note the heavy-weave jacket.

boat. I left Victoria and took the boat to Paris, from Paris I caught a train to Marseilles and from there took a ship for the East.

Naturally, being a proud Scot, I wore my kilt and cut quite a dashing figure as the ship sailed from Marseilles, complete with a contingent of French soldiers *en route* to one of their colonies, a place I had never heard of called Vietnam. To many of my contemporaries, the notion of leaving for a foreign land on Christmas Eve was quite a sad one, but I felt nothing but excitement, setting out on an adventure in the wide world to reach a place I had thought, talked and even dreamed about: Japan.

I did see quite a slice of the world on the journey as luck would have it. My accommodation was far from luxurious as I was travelling 4th class steerage, which involved sleeping on canvas on top of my suitcase. I broke the monotony of the journey by exercising every day, running around the decks and doing callisthenics, which caught the attention of the French officers. When we stopped at Port Said in Egypt, around the time of the Suez incident, I realized there were drawbacks to wearing a kilt, given the unpopularity of such attire with the local populace following their recent experience of the Black Watch, which had lead to President Nasser having them ejected. Since I had ambitions to reach Japan alive, I changed my kilt for the stopover; sometimes you just have to compromise!

Egypt was by no means a bad experience for me, even though it was a difficult time to be there. The French officers, who had taken a shine to me on the ship, were making a three-day excursion to see the pyramids and hired me to carry their bags, so I was able to earn a little extra money, learn a little French and get to see one of the seven wonders of the ancient world, all unexpected bonuses.

The ship's next port of call was Bombay, in India, where I was able to go to the YMCA and teach some judo. Bombay was also the first place I visited where I saw people lying dead in the street. It was shocking in the extreme but opened my eyes to so much of what we in the West take for granted. From Bombay, I worked as one fo the crew and enjoyed most of the rest of the trip, especially the stop overs in Singapore and Saigon, where I was also able to do some teaching. On the latter part of the trip, *en route* to Hong Kong, I even had the dubious pleasure of experiencing a typhoon.

We eventually arrived in Yokohama, Tokyo, on the 28 January 1958, and I was met by Richard 'Dickey' Bowen and Warwick Stepto.

Unlike many westerners, who had gone to Japan purely to get better at judo, I was there with a very clear idea in mind, planted there by T.P. Leggett, to achieve self-improvement too. Initially I stayed at the YMCA, then moved in with Dickey Bowen and Jonny Hateshita and began the regular pilgrimages to the Kodokan for judo practice.

THE JAPANESE EXPERIENCE

When I disembarked in Japan, it was a very different place to what it is today; it was like nowhere else on earth. Now it has succumbed to the strong westernizing forces that were beginning to operate on it even then and is like so many other industrialized countries. Perhaps the fact that there are eight million less adults practising judo on a regular basis is in some way indicative of this. Certainly the Japanese attitude is radically different to what it was forty yars ago, although some elements still remain.

When I arrived in Japan, I found the people to be exceptionally courteous and kind, but discovered that, in spite of their polite exteriors, they were phenomenally racist in outlook and attitude. The discrimination that exists there is purely on the basis of being Japanese or non-Japanese. As one apologist for his countrymen, who vigorously denied any hint of racism, explained, 'Black, white, Korean or

Chinese, we do not care, we do not discriminate between foreigners. Of course, you are not Japanese, that is true.'

The biggest surprise that I got as I found my feet in Tokyo was the discovery that I could not speak English, at least not in such a way that the Japanese who spoke English could understand. I rapidly developed a Sean Connery type Scottish accent, as it was important to be able to earn some money from teaching English in order to survive. I got very intensely involved in training and was surprised to discover that the average Japanese tended to regard the superb judo men I so admired as eccentrics, even almost lunatics. The success of Yasuhiro Yamashito in judo, over two decades later, has done much to transform this image. His winning ways have made him an enormously popular public figure. His obvious intelligence and integrity, combined with his articulate sincerity and friendliness, have made him a hero off the mat as well as on it. Even his build, which is by western standards rounded and chubby, fits the Japanese image of the mighty warrior, as mirrored in their traditional wrestling, sumo. Yamashita alone has done an enormous amount to restore the status of Japanese judo within Japanese society.

Life in Tokyo, in 1958, was diverse and exciting and a far cry from the port of Leith. I even got a job as an extra in a John Wayne movie, at one point. I soon gained the necessary confidence in my English to teach conversation classes. However, I never lost sight of the fact that I was there to do judo, even though in the first four months I never managed to throw anybody!

I slowly came to believe that the Japanese are very modish people and tend to be great trend followers rather than innovators, but their achievements in the later half of this century have been remarkable and would seem to belie this. At one time, 'Made in Japan' was synonymous with cheap, perhaps shoddy goods; in forty years this has been completely turned around and we now expect goods of the highest quality when we see that label. Japanese education is of an equally high order. Judo is an integral part of it and is compulsory in high school education, just as physical education is in Great Britain.

The Japanese are far from perfect. There is as much to criticize as there is to praise. Japanese society is both demanding of its own people and unfair to those of other nations. Their capitalist success is based on a kind of utilitarianism and social responsibility that verges on being what I can only call super communism. They have practised extreme forms of protectionism for years and got away with it and, in the final analysis, they seem only to be out for themselves. In my view, they are modern imperialists, conquering and colonializing by financial domination where they could not do so militarily. In common with Germany, they lost the war and are winning the peace.

I was lucky enough to be accepted totally by the Japanese, in a way that not many westerners are. One of the reasons for that was that I tried so hard at my judo while I was out there. I trained very hard and never allowed myself to be side-tracked. I learned to speak colloquial Japanese and, I believe, came to understand them as few westerners do. I was taken care of initially by Mr Osawa and Mr Daigo, who were both exceptional judo men and, after a short period of adjustment, I was taken by Warwick Stepto to begin training at Nichidai University.

The Japanese University System

At Nichidai I was introduced to the Japanese system for the first time and found it extremely difficult because I did not understand it. All of Japanese life is governed by status and position, the language is filled with indicators of the different levels of respect that are expected and required in everyday conversation. Age brings seniority and seniority is unchanging. The Japanese universities operate on a very strict *sempai-kohai* system. The *se-*

Fig 5   The 1959 line-up of the special students at the Kodokan. Among the faces are Toshiro Daigo – All-Japan Champion and now Chief Instructor at the Kodokan (front row, far right); Isao Inokuma, Olympic Champion in 1964 and World Champion in 1965 (front row, far left); Risei Kano, son of the founder of judo and President of the Kodokan (front row, centre), and George Kerr (back row, third from the right).

mpai is the senior student and the *kohai* the junior. The *kohai* are virtually slaves to the senior students, in much the same way as were the first years in the fagging system that used to operate in the English public schools. The system has its pros and cons. The *sempai* have considerable power over the *kohai* and, should they choose to abuse it, the consequences can be unpleasant. As a young *kohai* in my first year, I was a skivvy. I had to wash the senior students' kits, sweep the mats, brush floors and perform all the general chores that they required. In return, I and the other *kohai* would go on the mat and get beaten up!

It took a while for me to grasp the relationship which existed between *sempai* and *kohai* and I once came close to being lynched for throwing a bucket of cold water over one of my *sempai* in retaliation for a joke he had played on me the previous day. Such reprisals are not the Japanese way; the *kohai* has to grin and bear it and I was extremely unpopular for a while because of this inability to know my place. Life for a couple of years was very hard, but I gradually came to understand the system and was not treated any worse or better than anybody else, so it was bearable.

Once you become a second-year student, you are no longer the lowest of the low and you have *kohai* whom you can command. However, with power comes responsibility and the *sempai* are expected to look after the *kohai* and, of course, pay for everything

18

Fig 6(a)–(d)   George Kerr as uke again – this time for Shinohara, 4th dan, the captain of Meiji University, who is demonstrating his *tsuri-komi-goshi* in 1959.

(a)

(b)

(c)

Fig 7(a)–(c)   George Kerr demonstrating *nage-no-kata* with Yamagishi at the *Kakami Birake*, the annual opening ceremony of the Kodokan.

Fig 8   The Japanese national squad getting ready for an afternoon's practice at the Kodokan.

should they go out to eat or drink. I remember practising in Nagoya when I was a first-year student and a couple of strong third years decided to gang up on me because I was a *gaijin*, that is a foreigner. After a couple of drubbings, when one of them stepped up to carry on dishing out the punishment, my *sempai* Ozaki intervened, saying 'Try me' to a surprised would-be bully. The fourth-year students rule the roost, being answerable only to the *sensei* or teachers but the nature of the character-building training they underwent meant, at least in my day, that abuses were very infrequent and the system produced judo men of integrity, capable of thinking and acting correctly. It is a system that is ideally

suited to the conformist and indeed conformity would seem to be one of its main goals.

It is the university system in Japan which produces and maintains the champions of Japanese judo. There is a tendency for western athletes, who are often professional in all but name, to assume that the Japanese are also professional but in fact they remain for the most part true amateurs. They have to follow a four-year course at university doing judo, alongside a demanding course of academic study. At the end of their four years, they qualify to become high school judo teachers, or go into business, or become policemen, with a degree which, apart from its academic value, is proof that they have

Fig 9(a)   Nakanishi's hips are well across and the left-hand grip on the sleeve is clear in this attack on Dyot in the 1984 Olympic Games.

Fig 9(b)   The rotation required to throw the Frenchman is quite extreme as a result of Nakanishi having attacked with no grip on his opponent's judogi with the right hand. He has gripped Dyot's wrist instead. Dyot attempts to spin out, but the fall is a heavy one.

completed a course in character training second to none. The future of judo may well lie more in the area of education than in sport. Certainly, I got far more from my education in judo at a Japanese university than I would if I had participated only as a sportsman. It is worth nothing as well that Japanese society is the least violent in the industrialized world and the crime rate is the lowest. The contribution of judo to the socialization of its people should not be underestimated, although undoubtedly there are other factors involved. The student of judo acquires strong personal discipline and discipline is something people need; some things never change.

One point that has to be made at this stage is that the priorities of the western sportsman are different from that of the Japanese university judo student. Many western competititors come to Japan for short trips in order to get concentrated high-quality training, that will serve them in good stead when they fight in international tournaments. They look at the Japanese university system, together with their coaches, and inevitably criticize it. This is understandable, but their criticism is generally misconceived. Given the tradition, the facilities and the number of people doing judo in Japan, the Japanese ought to be unbeatable in international contest. Recent non-Japanese successes have clearly demonstrated that they are not and the question everyone asks is why? Western coaches point to their university system, and the shugyo (ascetic training) tradition that has always prevailed, and point to the fact that they over-train for the purposes of achieving tournament success. Also there is a widespread lack of expertise as regards non-traditional conditioning methods, such as weight-training.

Such factors have to be understood in context though. To the average Japanese *sensei*, the process of training is as important as the result and success in the Olympics or World Championships is not the aim. Such competitions only really matter to those few individuals who take part in them. The typical student wants to become good enough to get into the university team and the goal of the team is to win the All Japan University Championships. The level of such judo players is about that of medallists in a European Championship. As the students have to train every day, the rhythm and intensity of the practice is different to the kind that top western competitors undergo. The students are not clones, there is a huge difference in attitude amongst them. Some are self-confessed judo lunatics who think of nothing else but getting into the university team and graduate to become teachers themselves or join the police; others go to work for companies in careers which depend upon their academic achievements. Their lives at university are hard and many will bemoan their lot on a daily basis, but much of their moaning and groaning should not be taken at face value.

Of course, all Japanese judo teachers are not alike and some have made it their task to keep Japanese judo in the forefront, men like the 1973 World Champion, Nobuyuki Sato, who went on to produce great champions like Yamashita and Katsuhiko Kashiwazaki at Tokai University. These men are competitors and coaches of the highest calibre, who know all there is to know about preparing an athlete for judo competition. However, they are in the minority and there are many less able teachers in Japan who none the less think that they have seen, done and know as much.

The other major group doing judo in Japan, outside of the universities, are the police. For them, judo is part of their job and they have to do a minimum of two hours every day. However, many become like full-time amateurs and seem to lose both their inspiration and then their love for the study of judo. Over-saturation results in them preferring ground-work.

There are other kinds of judo club, which belong to Japanese companies. They provide the facilities for their employees because they value the health and recreational aspects that

Fig 10(a)–(d)   An *osoto-otoshi* by Akanoshi of Japan against Porscher of East Germany in the *Tournoi de Paris* of 1984.

Fig 10(a)   The Japanese fighter leaps in with an *osoto* attack, trapping the German's leg and pinning his weight on it. Note that the attack stemmed from Porscher being in an awkward defensive crouching posture, which Akanoshi has taken advantage of. As he makes the initial attack he has not taken a grip with his left hand.

Fig 10(b)   By bending his knees and hanging with his full body-weight on his opponent Porscher, Akanoshi has pulled the German into an unstable position and he has nowhere to go but down.

Fig 10(c) As he is tipped over, Akanoshi straightens both legs and springs upon his toes, all the while maintaining the pull with the hands. Note how the left arm controls the head and the right the sleeve.

Fig 10(d) Ippon. Akanoshi is in the perfect position to follow up with *kesa-gatame* in newaza, had the score been any less.

doing judo affords the practitioner. Such company facilities can be compared to company membership of health clubs and gymnasiums in the West. Again, however much time they spend on the mat, they are strictly amateurs.

TRADITION AND CHANGE

Judo is a profound subject. It is many things to many different people and, in some cases, affords a lifetime of study and learning. It has over eight million practitioners world-wide and, in the 1988 Olympic Games, participants for the judo event came from over 100 countries. It is a truly international sport, administered and managed by the International Judo Federation, and holds its own world championships every two years. Judo has expanded and developed quite remarkably in recent years, but, if it is to continue to thrive, it must continue to evolve and develop in a variety of areas. A commom complaint in Japanese dojos is that the western influence has spoiled the style of Japanese judo. 'That's not judo', is a complaint frequently heard there these days and the koka mentality of winning at all costs, regardless of aesthetic style, is felt by many Japanese to have diminished the art and, consequently, the aesthetic appeal of the activity has suffered.

Judo originated in Japan, from a synthesis of techniques and training methods from the old ju-jitsu schools and the educational philosophy of Professor Jigoro Kano. It is an activity that is in danger of forgetting its origins. The great appeal of modern judo lies in the sporting element, in the thrill of competition or *shiai* and the excitement of superbly trained athletes battling for gold medals. The exhilaration felt is similar to that of witnessing a boxing match or any other dynamic combat sport; there is an element of risk taking and the possibility of a complete reversal of fortunes is always there. A good judo match is a dramatic arena where anything might happen. The ancient Greeks, who invented drama, created within it the concept of *peripeteia* which is a dramatic reversal of fortunes usually in the form of a tragic fall (the central notion of high tragedy).

In judo competitions, such *peripeteia* abound, in spite of the fact that there has been a tendency in recent years for contests to become increasingly tactical as the margins between the skill levels and fitness of the various competitors have diminished. However, even the misguided alteration of the rules, particularly the introduction of the passivity ruling, which was intended to improve the sport's spectator appeal, but actually threaten to reduce judo to the level of mere wrestling, has not eradicated the all or nothing nature of *shiai*. Even the Olympic and World Championship medals continue to be decided by ippon throws in the most dramatic fashion. There is still hope for the future of judo, regardless of all the attendant problems.

TRADITIONAL JUDO: FROM SELF-DEFENCE TO 'THE WAY' AND ON TO SPORT

There is nothing wrong with deep involvement in the sporting aspect of judo, in fact the young world-class competitors are the cutting edge of the judo movement. Major technical advances only result from increasingly stiff opposition from difficult opponents. Nevertheless, having seen over forty years of judo, I cannot help but feel that obsession with sporting contest, which results in the exclusion of *kata* and other traditional aspects from training, is detracting from the overall appeal and value of the activity.

Competition employing all the violent battlefield techniques of the old ju-jitsu schools was felt to be impossible, simply because such techniques were designed purely for self-defence and, with that end in view, were calculated to injure and drastically disable any would-be assailant. As a result, training was

Fig 11   This is committed, skilled judo. All four feet are off the ground but Paul Sherls of Britain is in classic *ouchi-gari* position against Jukka-Pekka Metsola of Finland in the British Open 1987.

carried out by the practice of pair-form *kata*, which embodied the essence of the system's techniques and which honed the skills of the practitioners to perfection. The prevalence of the contest-orientated mind in dojos everywhere tends to lead to all aspects of judo which are not competition-based being devalued and even invalidated. The attitude can be summed up by the phrase, 'There is no point doing that, it does not happen in a contest', as if competitions were the be-all and end-all of judo. The pressure to be contest-effective all the time leads to a narrowing of focus and prevents a lot of people enjoying other aspects of judo. It also leads to a very hard style of practice, often concentrating on

Fig 12   The classical left *uchimata* performed by the great Yasuhiro Yamashita of Japan on Robert van de Walle of Belgium in the 1981 World Championships open category in Maastricht in Holland.

(a)

Fig 13(a) and (b)   Nobuyuki Sato, professor of judo at Tokai University and one of the leading figures in modern judo, demonstrating one of his favourite techniques – *sasae-tsuri-komi-ashi*.

Few randori partners the world over fail to be caught by *ashiwaza* of one kind or another, and generally they go over at least once to this *sasae-tsuri-komi-ashi*. Sato learned it from his older brother Nobuhiro (in itself, an example of a traditional method of Japanese judo teaching) and used it first as a teenager. It came in useful in his very last match when he beat Kazuhiro Ninomiya in the All-Japan Championships in 1974, at the late age of thirty.

In his masterly survey, *Ashiwaza, (De-Ashi-Barai, Okuri-Ashi-Barai, Harai-Tsuri-Komi-Ashi, Sasae-Tsuri-Komi-Ashi)*, published by Ippon/Crowood in 1990, he emphasizes the importance of smooth, flowing movement patterns. This promotes the kind of judo that allows practice well into advanced age.

(c)   Nobuyuki Sato is equally adept at *de-ashi-barai* on the left.

(b)

(c)

Fig 14   Totikachvilli, the superb Russian bantamweight world champion, throws Roux of France with an unorthodox but highly effective technique at the European Championships in Pamplona 1988. Note the use of coloured judogi.

frustrating the opponent and closing them down to prevent them doing judo rather than the creative, skilful interplay that *randori* ought to be.

Jigoro Kano demonstrated a vision akin to genius when he devised his system of Kodokan Judo, but it should never be forgotten that judo was derived from ju-jitsu. Kano trained in the Tenjin Shin'yo Ryu and the Kito Ryu and it was from these classical ju-jitsu schools that the majority of the techniques of modern judo derive. In more recent times, there has been an increase in the techniques of sport judo, largely as a result of the influence of Russian fighters coming into the sport with their own traditions of Sombo wrestling. This eclectic quality has always been judo's greatest strength. When confronted by anything new and of value, it has always been capable of assimilating it. For this reason it was always extremely useful for self-defence purposes because it remained an open-ended system. Kano sent special students from his Kodokan to go and train in other disciplines under Morihei Ueshiba, the founder of modern aikido and Gichin Funakoshi, the founder of the Shotokan karate school, in order that they should learn from these great teachers and bring their learning back to the Kodokan.

Judo is unusual because Professor Kano originally made provision for the study and practice of both striking and throwing techniques, in an effort to create a complete system of physical education and self-defence. Kodokan judo, in its earliest form, was virtually the study and practice of all-in fighting, with most of the techniques being inherited from the classical *ryu*. However, the practice of the aspects of judo which relate to self-defence, specifically *kata* and *atemi-waza*, have tended to be ignored in the frenzied promotion of the sport of judo, as much in Japan where social violence is not really a problem as in the West where it never ceases to be, if the media are to be believed.

Political considerations have also weighed heavily with judo's governing bodies. They have been concerned to distance themselves from the lunatic fringe of the martial arts whose involvement in sensationalist and sometimes illegal activities made any association undesirable. The importance of a clean image cannot be overstated, especially in a media-dominated culture where the majority of the public never get any closer to the activity than its projected image.

Kano himself had been aware of the importance of this over a hundred years earlier and dealt with the image problem of the time in a unique way. In the late nineteenth century, classical ju-jitsu was at the nadir of its fortunes and many of the best exponents were unable even to earn a living from teaching their craft. However, Kano perceived much of value in ju-jitsu, both in terms of its practical worth as a method of essentially unarmed self-defence and as a cultural artefact capable of embodying traditional values. Its main drawback was the bad image people had of it

and its practitioners and it was to fall to Kano to transform that image.

Currently, judo in Europe is practised almost exclusively as an Olympic sport. The majority of those who participate do so with a view to improving their performance in *randori*, where they attempt to throw, hold, strangle and armlock fully resisting training partners, who attempt to do the same to them. This method of practising pretty well duplicates the conditions of contest and so as preparation for the sport of judo is reasonably appropriate. However, Kano conceived his judo to be much more than a mere sport. It has often been said that, in typical Japanese eclectic fashion, he took what was best from the numerous ju-jitsu *ryu* to create his own more practicable system which he named judo.

This is essentially true but in fact he did far more than that. Of special significance was his choice of the characters *ju* and *do* which were to form the name of his new system. The first character, *ju* denotes flexibility and has connotations of the capacity for softness to overcome hardness, which was one of the concepts intrinsic to ju-jitsu from its inception. There is nothing innovative there but, combined with the second character, *do*, denoting 'way' or 'spiritual path', the combat system that was ju-jitsu became raised to a different level.

The late Donn F. Draeger, in his superb scholarly studies *Classical Budo* and *Classical Bu-Jutsu* (published by Weatherhill) explained the differences between 'budo' and 'bu jutsu' by describing the former as 'the classical art of self-perfection' and the latter as 'the classical art of self-protection'. This distinction holds the key to an understanding of why judo flourished when ju jitsu had teetered on the brink of oblivion. Ju jitsu was a product of a violent era. Although the name was given to the system of (virtually) unarmed fighting in the Tokugawa Shogunate, the techniques that comprised it were much older and were in fact battlefield-generated methods of

31

Fig 15 (a) and (b)   George Kerr's left *uchimata* – in 1979.

fighting without weapons, a last resort for the warrior who found himself disarmed. Practical effectiveness was the only criteria for the preservation and continued practice of such techniques, many of which can only be described as vicious and savage. This viciousness was a hallmark of classical ju jitsu techniques and totally acceptable as an aspect of a truly martial system, that is to say one designed for warfare. However, these same qualities served to discourage people from practising ju jitsu in the modern period, the late nineteenth century, which was a much more civilized and peaceful time.

Fortunately, Kano recognized this and went to great pains to present his new system to the general public as a system of great cultural worth which, while having a certain practical usefulness in terms of self-defence, was more importantly an effective method of physical education, based upon strong ethical tenets, Kano's strongly developed philosophies made his judo very attractive and appealing to his countrymen who were then, as now, preoccupied by the necessity for self-improvement, and there was an explosion of interest.

Perhaps today the majority of typical judoka are not so high-minded and idealistic as the original students of Kano's Kodokan (literally 'the school for studying the way'). This may be largely due to the emhasis placed on sporting competition to the exclusion of other factors. Most judoka see their sport as a good way of keeping fit which doubles as a usable method of self-defence, although few would deny that judo practice helps with the socialization process and improves one's self-control almost as a matter of course.

Fig 16   George Kerr in the weights room of the Edinburgh Club.

I now run my own judo school in Edinburgh, The Edinburgh Club, and I see the future of judo as being very much linked to education. When I lived in Japan, I tried to understand the Japanese mind, and I accepted their structures and conditioning. When I returned to Great Britain, I was more Japanese than Scots; I always tried hard to do good upright judo, whatever the circumstances. I was skilful by any standards and could do *kata* and continued to study judo. Now I have seen thirty years of change and developments, not all positive, and feel that the balance is in many areas wrong and needs to be restored.

The German philosopher, Hegel, wrote of the process by which we learn and develop in our lives and devised a model of thesis, antithesis and synthesis. If traditional judo is the thesis and the development of sport judo the antithesis, our task for the future should be to combine and synthesize the best that we can from two apparently irreconcilable positions, however ingrained they may seem to be with cultural prejudices. This is an issue that all of those involved in judo must begin to address sooner rather than later, and hopefully this book will go some way towards beginning that task.

2 The Western Tradition:
Judo for Sport by Peter Seisenbacher

Unlike my coach, George Kerr, who grew up in judo within an essentially classical, traditional system, my background is one of contest after contest, a struggle to be the best, which at times it seemed would never end. Judo for me was a sport first and last and the ultimate goal was always to win an Olympic gold medal. I had no sense of it as an educational vehicle for self-development and really it did not become that for me until I became the Olympic Champion; my obsession with winning and being the best was too great to be diverted by philosophy.

I began doing judo at the age of eight. I always enjoyed doing it, just practising for its own sake, finding satisfaction in the rough and tumble and the physical training. I enjoyed contest even more, which was perhaps why I was always stronger in that situation, harder to beat than in practice. This was true throughout my career. I remember fighting the Japanese competitor, Myoshi, in the Europe vs. Asia match in 1985. We had practised together a lot at Tokai University when I had trained in Japan and he had given as good as he got, throwing me quite regularly. I armlocked him in 10 seconds in our match. When he returned to Tokai, he told the other Japanese there that, 'He is different in contest'.

I have fought hundreds, perhaps thousands, of contests in my career but some of the clearest memories I have are of my early rivals, who were equally my early heroes, men I sought to both emulate and defeat such as Detlef Ultsch of East Germany and Bernard Tchoullyan of France. Ultsch threw me many times. I could not make him bend and, whenever I attacked, he simply picked me up. He was a squat powerful fighter and a worthy World Champion. After numerous defeats, I eventually caught up with him in the Potsdam Tournament. He picked me up and threw me three times for minor scores, but my *newaza* had grown strong and I eventually armlocked him with *juji-gatame*. However, Tchoullyan was the fighter I never managed to beat. His left *ippon-seoi-nage* was incredibly fast and skilful. In one tournament, someone took a photograph of him throwing me with *ippon-seoi-nage*, which was used in a promotional judo calendar. He retired before I reached full maturity so I never got my revenge on him for putting me in the calendar! There were so many hard fighters at under 86k in Europe that the European Championships were always of an exceptionally high standard. Tchoullyan, who was World Champion, never won it. One man who won it three times, and was always a major problem for me, was the Russian, Pesniak, but more of him later.

TECHNICAL PROGRESS

In the early days, the hallmark of my judo was to grip and hurl myself into the attack with a strong pull and the abandonment of youth which allowed me to throw quite a few of my opponents. However, as the level at which I competed got higher, it became increasingly difficult to make these techniques work and I

Fig 17(a) and (b)   In the European Championships in Rostock, in 1982, Seisenbacher took a score from the world champion, Bernard Tchoullyan (France).

Fig 18 One of Seisenbacher's great rivals from the early part of his career, the brilliant French champion, Bernard Tchoullyan, throws another great fighter Detlef Ultsch of East Germany with a superb left *ippon-seoi-nage*. This is a classic finish to a classical technique; note how straight Tchoullyan's legs are and how far forwards he is bent. A remarkable technique worth comparing to the drop *seoi-nage* so popular in modern judo.

are just evading the issue. The real solution to the problem is to analyse your own strengths and weaknesses and first get the judo right. Strength or fitness, if they are the weak point, can be more easily remedied. Strengthening the technical base of the judo has to take priority and the majority of training time should be devoted to that.

I was exceptionally fortunate to have the guidance of my coach, George Kerr, a man whose understanding of judo and of the judo-ka's mind is unsurpassed. The majority of to-day's judo players, though, have to find their own way and are not as lucky as I was. Even though there are many good coaches, there are many more players in need of proper guidance than there are receiving it.

It is very important for all judo players to keep an open mind and be receptive to new ideas and possibilities. When I first went to Japan in 1980, having won a silver medal in the European Championships, I thought I was quite strong, and was there for three months training with my eye on the World Championships in Maastricht the following year. I was truly shocked by how many strong training partners were available in Japan. Every other person I practised with seemed that they might be capable of winning a medal in a European Championships.

The way I practised proved to be exhausting too. My judo was based on tension and condition. It comprised strong gripping, explosive techniques, then more tension. In dojos in Austria or elsewhere in Europe, I could maintain it for an hour or an hour and a half, but against fairly strong opposition in Japan, it was a very different story. In the protracted Japanese training sessions, routinely lasting two and a half to three hours, it was just too exhausting to practise this way. No one could have been fit enough to keep it up. I would fade badly towards the end of training sessions and would then risk the danger of getting injured through being exhausted. Therefore, I had to change my style. I found myself fighting less and less at the close-range

was countered more frequently. Therefore, I had to modify what I did so that it would be effective even against the strongest opposition. Many medium-strength judoka, when they confront this kind of difficulty, regard improving their physical condition as the answer, working on their fitness and perhaps trying to get stronger through weight-training. Others change weight categories in the hope that their judo will fare better against a different set of opponents. Any of these may be valid strategies in some cases, but often they distance, where the opponent is under immediate and constant pressure, because so too was I. More and more, I got used to fighting from the classical distance, as most of the Japanese did.

The major advantage of this style of fighting and practice was that it gave me more space and time to react to the numerous fast and low attacks so prolific in Japanese dojos. It also made me learn to defend in an upright posture and to use hip movement and mobility rather than stiff arms, which rapidly became exhausted, to defend. As my confidence in this kind of mobile defence grew, my ability to relax and save energy as I practised, and then use it more efficiently, increased greatly. This should not be misunderstood as meaning that I learnt to coast, or practise in a lazy way; the practice remained intense and equally demanding, requiring considerable concentration. The major difference was that I stopped wasting energy needlessly and developed a more confident and economical style.

Success in judo does not come quickly. My silver medal in the 1980 European Championships at the tender age of twenty had been an early high point in front of a home crowd in Vienna. I had won my way to the final by the skin of my teeth. As an example, in the semi final I fought the experienced Englishman, Peter Donnelly, who was a very skilful thrower. He threw me for waza-ari, yuko and koka and three times had me in *osaekomi*. Fortunately, his *newaza* was every bit as bad that day as his *tachiwaza* was strong and I escaped three times. In the last minute, when he was content to defend to hold onto his lead and a seemingly sure place in the final, I had a flash of inspiration and threw him for ippon with *ouchi-gari*. Such things happen in judo, although they do not happen as a matter of course.

It was to be another three years before I would win another medal in the European Championships, and six years before I would finally win a European gold medal at under 86k in the 1986 Championships in Belgrade

in Yugoslavia. However, speaking truthfully, the European Championships were never my major goal. In the early 1980s, the only thing that really mattered was the Los Angeles Olympic games. George Kerr attached no importance to the fact that I took only silver in 1983 and bronze in 1984 at the European Championships; they were just training events for the Olympic Games.

Many judoka, once they are beaten in a major event, do not really recover because their confidence is damaged. Psychologically, they have to believe that they are invincible and cannot cope when their own myth is shattered. George would tell me that the European Championships were only a yardstick, that anyone capable of winning a medal at them just might do the same at the World Championships or Olympic Games. He also pointed out that people who won the European title may often have peaked then and would be disappointed at the more important events. Therefore, we trained and prepared with this in mind. When I lost it was because I was not as well prepared as I could have been, but we had decided that, in order to win the war, it was not necessary to win every battle on the way.

The career of Neil Adams, who had arrived on the international scene a few years before me and whom I admired enormously for his spectacularly skilful judo, was one of my inspirations and his career makes a most interesting contrast with my own. He won the European title in 1980, but lost in the Olympic final to Enzio Gamba of Italy. He won the European Championships again in 1983 and 1984 and 1985, but was thrown for ippon in the 1984 Olympic final in Los Angeles by Frank Wieneke of West Germany. This was a huge upset, but not a fluke, Wieneke was always potentially Adams' most dangerous opponent. If Adams had had George Kerr for his coach, I think he would have been Olympic champion but, as it was, he was unlucky.

In 1988, in the European Championships in Pamplona, prior to the Seoul Olympics, I was

Fig 19(a) and (b)   One of the Soviet Union's most formidable middleweights, Vladimir Iastkevich, threw Seisenbacher for ippon with *osoto-gari*, one of his own favourite techniques in the final of the European Championships in Vienna in 1980.

Fig 20   In the World Championships in Maastricht in 1981. David Bodavelli threw Seisenbacher with this fine *uranage* for waza-ari. Seisenbacher was preparing to break-fall as he flew through the air.

Fig 21   Seisenbacher's favourite position at the start of ground-work – this time in the European Championships in Belgrade – hunting for the armlock.

Fig 22   The intensity of Seisenbacher's personal coach, George Kerr, who is fighting from the mat side.

Fig 23 Much of George Kerr's training time in Japan was spent at Tokai University just outside Tokyo. The judo professor there was Nobuyuki Sato, manager of the Japanese national squad for over ten years.

(a)

Fig 24 (a) and (b) World champion and winner of the All-Japan Championships, he was known as 'Newaza Sato' because of the strength of his groundwork. However, he was also particularly respected for his *ashiwaza*. Here he demonstrates one of his favourite techniques, *sasae-tsuri-komi-ashi*, which he used to do in combination with *osoto-gari*. Even in his forties, he remains a formidable practice and an inspiration for successive generations of judoka from Japan and the rest of the world.

(b)

Fig 25   Yasuhiro Yamashita is the most successful judo competitor Japan has ever produced. Olympic and world champion, he won the coveted All-Japan Championships no fewer than nine times and was unbeaten for almost a decade until his retirement in 1985. He was a student at Tokai University during his years of international competition, and so was a regular face in the dojo. He now teaches at the University himself.

Fig 26   Although a big man – his fighting weight was 127k – Yamashita embodies classical Japanese judo. Even in competitions he always took the formal sleeve/lapel grip and launched his attacks from there. His range was wide but he concentrated on *uchimata*, *ouchi-gari*, *sasae-tsuri-komi-goshi*, and holds and strangles on the ground. However, his favourite throw has always been *osoto-gari*. In this demonstration he shows the beauty of traditional judo. Note his own perfect balance and the clean control of his opponent; he achieved this in contest too.

Fig 27 January 1984, *Tournoi de Paris*.
Seisenbacher was trying out new techniques –
and new fashions, although the moustache did
not last long.

well beaten by Densign White of Great Britain
who had learned how to get under my defence
with his superb *seoi-nage*. However, had we
met in Seoul, I am totally confident that I
would have beaten him and likewise the Russian, Vladimir Chestakov, who had earned his
selection for Seoul by winning against me
through scoring a koka in the Hungary Cup
just before the Olympics. If I ever met such
good fighters in anything but top mental and
physical condition they could beat me, but in
top form I was a very different proposition,
and that was how I always aimed to be for
World and Olympic Championships.

Defeat in what we considered lesser competitions was never a problem for me, largely
owing to the influence of George. Jigoro Kano
himself had something to say on the subject
that all judo players should read:

'Training in judo is also extremely beneficial
to those who lack confidence in themselves
due to past failures. Judo teaches us to look
for the best possible course of action, whatever the individual circumstances, and helps
us to understand that worry is a waste of energy. Paradoxically, the man who has failed
and the one who is at the peak of success are
in exactly the same position. Each must decide what he will do next, choose the course
that will lead him to the future. The teachings
of judo give each the same potential for success. In the former instance, guiding a man
out of lethargy and disappointment to a state
of vigorous activity.'

THE 1984 OLYMPIC GAMES

Many people imagine that, in doing anything
twice, even winning an Olympic gold medal,
the first time must be somehow more satisfying but, in my case, nothing could be further
from the truth. Despite the apparent sameness
of both events, I see them as quite different
and separate achievements. The first medal
was won by the early Seisenbacher, a pristine
judo fanatic and an athlete at the height of his
powers. The approach had been totally single-
minded and my dedication to the idea of becoming the Olympic Champion was realized
by an unrivalled but blinkered intensity. In
1984, I wanted to be an Olympic Champion
to the exclusion of everyone and everything
else. Nothing else mattered and I had no concept of a future beyond the Olympic final. I
had trained so hard and prepared so completely I felt I could not be beaten. The competition was to be everything. In 1984, I had
perfected my approach to contest. My aim
was to finish every fight as quickly as possible,
especially the earlier ones and so save energy
for the later, harder bouts.

Many people try to save their energy by not

giving 100 per cent against fighters that they do not feel threatened by. This is a mistake because often their opponent ends up scoring, then fighting a defensive contest and trying to hang on to their lead, which results in the other fighting burning up a lot more energy than he or she would have if an effort had been made to go all out for ippon from the beginning.

In the Los Angeles Olympics, I despatched Stanko Lopatic of Yugoslavia and then Chou Chung Chang of Chinese Taipei, for ippon in less than 2 minutes, confident that my next opponent would be the Japanese, Seki Nose. Nose had beaten me, very decisively, in the World Championships the previous year, but I had devised a strategy which depended upon giving him no chance to attack. The match with Nose was seen by many people to be highly controversial; it certainly was unusual the way it resolved itself. The pattern of the contest was that I would attack Nose who would block and then try to get on my back to attack with *newaza*, but I was too strong for Nose to keep on the ground, so he would then stand up and matte would be called. I was prepared to do this for the duration of the contest because I knew that, if he had no chance to attack, I could win.

The refereeing was not of a high standard and sometimes matte was called when it should not have been and sometimes it was not called when it should have been. The latter is what ended Nose's hopes of a gold medal. I had attacked him with *harai-goshi*, and fallen to the ground; he had jumped on my back. He tried to do a *shimewaza* and I stood up with him on my back, catching his foot with my nand as I did so. As I stood, I rolled him over my back and he assumed that there would be a call of matte as I had stood up from ground-work, as indeed there should have been. Therefore, when he rolled on his back and I dived on top of him he did not begin to struggle because he thought there was no danger. However, the referee did not call matte and I clamped on a solid *kami-shiho-gatame*. I remember laughing to myself as Nose moaned in English, 'Oh, no!', but there was no way I would have let him go or would have ever made the same mistake that he had. When I was in contest, the referee had to tell me twice when he called matte.

In the semifinal against Fabien Canu of France, I again won by ippon and found myself in the final against the American World Bronze Medallist, Bobby Berland of the USA. The home crowd had high hopes for their man and really believed, as he did, that they might win their first ever judo gold medal in their own back-yard. However, I spoiled their plans by throwing him for ippon with *tai-otoshi* early in the contest. I had really done it, the training and single-mindedness had paid off in the best possible way that I could then imagine. I had realized every competitor's dream: winning a gold medal in the Olympic Games.

The response in Austria to my becoming an Olympic Champion was incredible and I was not prepared for the fruits of success anything like as well as I had been prepared for tournaments. I was the first Austrian Olympic Gold Medallist at a summer Games in twenty-six years. From having been an almost anonymous amateur sportsman, doing a little-known and even less understood sport, I was on national television, rubbing shoulders with the rich and famous. I won Austria's sports personality of the year award, ahead of Nicki Lauder, the racing driver.

From being someone who had spent so long virtually unnoticed on the fringe of society, I was thrown into the limelight and I was forced to become adept at handling the attention and recognition, which for so many sports players turns into the apparent loss of any right to a private life. The limelight can harden into a glare of unwanted publicity and then there are very different problems which have to be managed.

I had so much to learn and so little time to learn it in, if the dream was not be transformed into a nightmare. At this point in my career, I was again indebted to George Kerr for the correct guidance and understanding which only he was in a position to be able to give me.

THE 1988 OLYMPIC GAMES

When I set my sights on a second Olympic gold, I wanted to prove something more important than what I had done the first time. I wanted to show that it was possible to win the Olympic title but be more than just a judo animal, a fighting machine programmed to win. After Los Angeles, I had developed enormously as a person and had cultivated a wide range of social skills and interests outside judo. I was quite a changed individual to the one who had defeated all before him in the 1984 Olympics. The strength that I had built in 1984 carried me right through the competitions of 1985 and into 1986 but I was no longer training as hard as I had done in order to win the Olympic gold. In a sense, as an athlete and a fighter, I was past my prime, many players thought I was over the hill, but in my own mind I remained the Champion and, although I recognized that I was not as strong in judo terms as I had been in 1984, I was not about to let just anyone assume the crown. Before each contest, I went out thinking. 'I am not going to lose against this guy because he's not good enough to beat me; he's not the personality I am'.

In 1986, I won the European title at last, beating Ben Spykers of Holland in the final. I was feeling quite strong at that time and so I entered the open category as well because I wanted to test myself against the big men of the sport. It was very enjoyable fighting the giants because most of them, despite their tremendous power and size, were not quite fast enough to deal with me effectively. I beat Elvis Gordon of Great Britain with a *ko-uchi-gari*, when he tried to pick me up with one of his famed dustbin counter throws. However, in the final against the East German champion, Henry Stohr, I lost through injury, damaging my knee in my zeal to defeat a much bigger opponent.

Before 1984, an injury would have been a disaster for me, a cause of depression and black moods but, with my new interests and responsibilities, I discovered it was no more than a nuisance. I had developed a new perspective since becoming Olympic Champion, along with the realization that there was more to life than judo. If I had met a brain surgeon or a composer before the Olympic Games I would have thought, 'He doesn't look so strong, I could beat him easily', with no thought for his particular talents or abilities. Everything was reduced to the basic ability to fight. Two years afterwards, I could meet people for what they were and not have to compare myself with them in that way.

The Seoul Olympic Games were to be my swan-song in international judo competition and I was determined that I should go out on a high note. I had missed the 1987 World Championships through being injured and had done poorly in the 1987 and 1988 European Championships, both times losing to the eventual silver medallist, Densign White of Great Britain, although in 1988 I did manage a bronze by armlocking Luc Suplis of Belgium in 28 seconds with *juji-gatame*. I had almost armlocked White the previous year but had been over-zealous, continuing to try and apply the armlock after the referee called matte when we rolled out of the area, which earned me a penalty and gave White the match. It made me aware of the importance of control.

George reminded me that the European Championships were a minor event in the scheme of things and losing there did not really matter, which put less stress on me. I continued to develop outside of judo, improving my communication skills and my knowledge of my own country's culture, music, art and history and learned to interact with people from different strata of society. Many people in Austrian judo were worried that I was not the fighter I had been before; the new socialized

Peter Seisenbacher who could laugh and joke about defeat worried them. Kurt Kucera, the President of the Austrian Federation, even urged me to revert to type saying, 'You've changed too much, you must go back to your old ways', but I wanted to go forwards not backwards, and so that was what I did.

The competition structure of the European events had changed and now involved holding the preliminaries on one day then, after a day's rest, weighing in again in order to fight the finals. This did not suit me as it was always hard work for me to make the weight even once. It also favoured the tactical fighters who fought long drawn-out contests, as it allowed them to rest for a day before fighting the finals. However, the Olympics retained the traditional format in which victory and defeat were all decided in one day, one toss of the dice, winner takes all. This is very much in keeping with the traditional spirit of judo and it suited me down to the ground.

Many people thought I was over the hill, and the pre-event favourites were Fabien Canu of France and Vladimir Chestakov of the Soviet Union. Ten weeks before the Games, Chestakov had beaten me by a koka in the Hungary Cup, guaranteeing his selection for Seoul, but it was only then that I had really begun to train. George Kerr had told me that the great boxing champion, Mohammed Ali, had always said ten weeks is the maximum it takes to get ready for a fight. He also knew what it took to motivate me and did just that, helping me to peak psychologically as well as physically at just the right time. This, of course, is only effective if you have been at the top for some time but, in general, it is true that a fighter in reasonable condition can be at his best in ten to twelve weeks, and when the day came I was.

My draw was good and I threw my first opponent, Claude Bonnet of Puerto Rico, for ippon in the first minute to save energy. Next was the Korean, Kim, a hard and seasoned fighter, eager to perform well in front of his home crowd, but I gave him no chance,

throwing him for ippon with *osoto-gari*. My third contest was to be against my old rival, the Frenchman Canu. I knew I would beat him. Canu was a crafty, cagey sort of fighter, very tactical and not keen to take risks. He often played the edge of the mat, and very successfully, but that was my territory too. It is easy to make people nervous on the edge and cause them to make mistakes. That was what I did with him and, threatening with *osoto-gari*, I switched to *tai-otoshi*, bowling him over for a yuko. Although I still believe in going for ippon, I also know that it is folly to throw away victory and so I let Canu come to me knowing I could handle his best attacks. This proved to be the right formula because I won and went through to the semifinal against Akinobu Osako of Japan.

In some ways, Osako was my most dangerous opponent. A classical judo man, he was capable of throwing anyone on the day. He had once very nearly thrown the mighty Yamashita in the All Japan Championships, although he had never been particularly successful againt foreign judoka. However, in Seoul he had despatched all of his opponents with stylish *uchimata* and *seoi-otoshi* attacks for ippon, until he met me. We were fairly evenly matched: he very upright and looking for the chance to throw for ippon, I more cautious and waiting to punish any lapse of concentration of error. Half-way through the match, I caught him with *osoto-gari* and scored yuko. Just as with Canu, I knew that I had won from the moment I scored and, sure enough, I withstood Osako's best efforts and again emerged the winner.

Now the arguments were raging around the stadium, was I going to confound tradition, superstition and opposition and become the first man to win two Olympic gold medals? Frank Wieneke had come close to it the day before but had been thrown quite unexpectedly for ippon with 13 seconds left on the clock in his final with Waldemar Legien of Poland. Even superstition seemed to conspire against the possibility.

Fig 28   Podium delight in Seoul after Seisenbacher won his second consecutive Olympic gold medal.

My opponent in the final was the Russian, Vladimir Chestakov, and the match was a hard-fought battle. I won by applying continuous pressure. Chestakov wanted to play it safe. He did not want to throw away an Olympic gold medal by risking all and going for ippon. We were even up until the last minute, but the advantage was mine. I had been there before and so I stepped up the pace, attacking and almost scoring with *osoto-gari* and *tani-otoshi*, earning a unanimous decision and a second Olympic gold medal, the first judoka in history to do so. I had proven to myself and to everyone else that it was possible to become Olympic Champion *and* have a life outside judo.

LIFE AS A PROFESSIONAL

Now I am a sports professional in Austria and my boss is the Minister for Sport. My work is no longer just performing judo, but also includes promoting it. This involves everything from organizing national judo days to getting people involved and giving them a taste of the sport, as well as liaising with representatives of big companies and trying to tie up sponsorship deals. My success has made me something of a role model for Austrian youngsters. Partly because of the publicity judo has received on account of my Olympic victories, there are now over 40,000 youngsters doing judo in Austria.

My task is not to win gold medals myself any longer but to enable others to do so, and also to educate the public as to what judo involves, what it is all about. For so many people, it is more than just a sport, and it has so much to offer.

PROGRESS AND DEVELOPMENT IN THE WEST

One thing that is now beyond dispute is that judo is no longer exclusively the domain of the Japanese. Many westerners have taken on their finest exponents and beaten them in international competitions of the most competitive nature, such as the World Championships and the Olympic games, and continue to do so. In the 1988 Games in Seoul in South Korea, on the very doorstep of Japan, there was a resounding victory over Japanese domination. In the best tradition of Holland's Anton Geesink, one *gaijin* after another stepped up to wrest the medals from the grasp of Japan's finest judo players. No fewer than four Japanese reigning World Champions were convincingly defeated. Only Hitoshi Saito prevented the unthinkable, grimly hanging onto his Olympic over 95k title, to ensure that one gold medal at least went home to the land of the rising sun. European judoka took eighteen of the twenty-eight medals in the men's event, a rout in judo terms.

The average Japanese judoka finds this sort of thing very hard to understand, still believing that their champions are the best and most skilful exponents of the art. The Japanese did better the following year in the 1989 World Championships in Yugoslavia, but the damage done to the myth of their invincibility in 1988 at the Olympic judo event corresponded to a Force 9 aftershock on the Judo Richter Scale, twenty-four years after Geesink's original earthquake.

The continuing success of non-Japanese competitors in international tournaments has created something of a dichotomy which, I believe, the Japanese mind finds hard to cope with, and which leads many Japanese judo teachers to make very curious pronouncements about what is and what is not judo. What the average Japanese perhaps fails to realize, which might help them to understand the reasons for western and in particular European successes, is the extent that the tradition of athletic and sporting competition in the west has been an influence.

Judo is a relatively new phenomenon on the world sporting stage. The techniques it utilizes go back centuries but the activity itself is really only a little over a century old. However, the Olympic Games, although resurrected by Baron de Courbertin as recently as 1896, within a decade of the genesis of judo, none the less represent an inheritance of sporting contest which began with the ancient Greeks over two and a half millennia ago. The original Games were held from 776 BC to 394 AD and represented over a thousand years of winning and losing, of competition between champions to crown the greatest of champions, and a competitive state of mind that has continued to the present day. The renaissance in enthusiasm for things classical, and the neo-classical movements in art and literature, all contributed to making the rebirth of the Olympic Games a reality, in preparing the European mind to be receptive to the idea. In the first modern Olympics, only six countries took party. The growth since that date has been astonishing.

Therefore, the concepts of contest and championship, of striving and winning are intrinsic to the western psyche. The competitive ethos enshrined by the modern games is at the heart of the successes of western athletes in modern judo. Although it took some time for western participants to familiarize themselves with the rules and customs of the Japanese sport, this capacity to compete, to respond to the gauntlet thrown down, ought not to be underestimated. The Olympics are also a special case and probably no occidental athlete is ever more highly motivated than for that one occasion every four years when the chance presents itself to be the best that there is.

There is also the factor of the differing pressures on the competititors to be considered, which does influence their eventual performances. I believe that the non-Japanese fighter competes out of a desire to win; the Japanese fighter out of a duty to win.

The Modification of Classical Techniques

The nature of competition has lead to a steady evolution in the kind of techniques that one sees used in contest in modern judo. The classical techniques of the Gokyo, such as *osoto-gari*, *harai-goshi*, *uchimata*, *seoi-nage* and *tai-otoshi*, never really go out of fashion, but are always capable of being effective if practised regularly and well honed for competition. However, they are rarely seen in the classical ideal form, although it has to be said that one of the things which made Yasuhiro Yamashita such an exceptional champion was the fact that he had no new or trick techniques, but rather performed the classic textbook techniques. He could be described as the incarnation of classical judo knowledge, so often did he perform perfect judo in high-level matches.

The distinguishing characteristic of western judo is that it does not aspire to the perfect form embodied in the Gokyo, but rather adapts it and modifies it to be more effective at throwing the opponent. The Japanese traditionalist school of thought argue that their goal is not, in fact, the same, since the aesthetic element is of intrinsic importance to the performance of any technique and if the use of force is excessive, rather than truly rational, then the object has not been achieved in accordance with the basic philosophical tenets of judo.

Compare this example of *osoto-gari*, which conforms to the ideal of correct technique and rational use of force found in the Gokyo, with the kind of modification that becomes necessary in the heat of contest, as seen in the sequence taken from the contest betwen Seisenbacher and Gheorghi Petrov (*see* Fig 30), where the standard form is radically altered in order to achieve the same result, that of putting the opponent flat on his back. The Gokyo version could only be performed with any certainty of success against an opponent with little or no knowledge of judo. I believe that, in this day and age, as far as competition is concerned, it has to be seen principally as an exercise in mechanics, a model to help the beginner understand the basics of gripping, throwing and controlling the fall of a co-operating partner.

Fig 29(a)–(d)   *Uchimata makikomi* by the Japanese, Tatsuto Mochida against Olivier Schaffter of Switzerland.

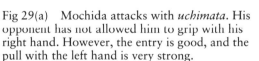

Fig 29(a)   Mochida attacks with *uchimata*. His opponent has not allowed him to grip with his right hand. However, the entry is good, and the pull with the left hand is very strong.

Fig 29(b)   To make the technique effective, Mochida has to spring up with his legs and *makikomi*. Schaffter attempts to defend by pushing the Japanese out with his left hand and straightening his back.

Fig 29(c)   Mochida reaches for the ground with his right hand, which negates Schaffter's attempt to defend with his left arm and causes him to overstretch. Mochida keeps turning to his left in a classic *makikomi* action to roll the Swiss fighter over his hip.

Fig 29(d)   Schaffter is thrown flat on his shoulders for ippon.

Fig 30(a)–(e)   The final of the World Championships u86k category in Seoul, South Korea, in 1985. Gheorghi Petrov of Bulgaria is attacked by Seisenbacher with left *osoto-gari*. The following sequence illustrates many of the classic points about attacking with *osoto-gari*; the hands and feet are working together, the attacker has achieved good head control, and his total commitment to the technique, in the all or nothing spirit of self-abandonment, is apparent.

Fig 30(a)   Seisenbacher has attacked Petrov's rear leg and he desperately tries to defend by stepping back on his right foot, but his weight is completely pinned over his trapped left knee. The control of the upper body and head is excellent.

Fig 30(b)   Seisenbacher compensates for Petrov's defence by hopping on his right foot and bending at the waist, pulling the Bulgarian's head down as he gets into a virtually unstoppable throwing position. Petrov attempts to defend by putting down his left hand, but the grip on the sleeve at the biceps controls his elbow.

Fig 30(c)   As Seisenbacher reaps back with his left leg, he turns his upper body into the downwards action of the throw. The strong pull with the right hand pulls Petrov's defending arm away from underneath, rendering it ineffective and the rotation of the upper body drives his opponent into the mat.

Fig 30(d) Ippon. An incontrovertible full point as Petrov is thrown flat on the back of his shoulders with impetus. Note the trained reflexes of a world-class fighter, the right hand reaching around the waist throughout the course of the throw looking for the chance to counter with a pick up.

Fig 30(e) The classic finishing position for a Seisenbacher throw, his hip on his opponent's head, the opponent flat on his back.

(a)

(b)

The Classical Method of Demonstrating Osoto-Gari *Fig 31(a)–(f)*

Fig 31(a) Tori takes a large step forward on his right foot, keeping the hips low by bending the right knee. He simultaneously pulls uke's left arm in to his body and unbalances uke by controlling his head with his left-hand grip on the lapel.

Fig 31(b) As the hands pull uke off-balance, the left hip swings through and the left leg begins to sweep back against uke's left leg. Uke's weight is pinned over his left foot.

Fig 31(c) Tori throws uke by pulling with the right arm, pushing with the left, reaping his legs off the ground with a powerful action of the left leg while all the time bending forward at the waist.

Fig 31(d) Leaning forward into the technique by bending at the waist ensures that tori avoids being countered as it prevents uke from shifting his balance to block or counter the attack. Tori is in the classic controlling position, balanced on his right supporting leg as he uses his hands to control uke's fall and guides him onto his back on the mat.

Fig 31(e) Uke is thrown flat on the back of his shoulders for a decisive ippon.

Fig 31(f) The classic finish: tori retains his balance rather than falling on top of his opponent as would be normal in contest. Note the pointed toes.

Without the cooperation of the partner, who in the instance described does not resist, it seems there are very few sets of circumstances in which such a technique would work. The supporters of traditional Japanese judo might wish to refute this and perhaps, occasionally, it does succeed with exceptionally gifted competitors. However, in the West, a much greater percentage of those actually participating in judo want to achieve success, to become winners, than in Japan where many people practise without that interest in contest.

(c)

(d)

(e)

(f)

The Japanese way is to persevere even if something seems demonstrably impractical or unsuitable. Sometimes this persistence pays off and sometimes not but, in either case, it requires a long time. The westerner wants quicker, more immediate, results. Instant gratification is the order of the day. The western competitor or coach, rather than flogging a dead horse, will tend to search out the quickest way to achieve the desired results. The key to success in modern judo in a competitive environment really lies betwen these two extremes. Judo is an inherently difficult activity and no one, however gifted, succeeds without a lot of hard work; the balance may be as radical as 10 per cent inspiration and 90 per cent perspiration.

Osoto-gari was always a favourite technique of mine when I was a competitor, in part because, with my long arms and legs, I could attack effectively from a distance but, although I had considerable success with it, I was forced to adapt it considerably in order to maintain this success.

Seisenbacher's Osoto-Gari *Fig 32(a)–(m)*
This sequence illustrates some of the points referred to in this chapter and, although the final technique is still called *osoto-gari*, it is a very different technique to the classical version found in the Gokyo. Of particular note is the sequence of moves which allow me to get my preferred grip for the technique, which is, if not unorthodox, at least uncommon. Gripping, in fact, is one area where the average western competitor can still learn a lot from watching and practising the Japanese: it is one of their areas of great strength.

Fig 32(a)   A fairly typical *kenka-yotsu* situation, tori grips uke's right lapel at the level of his collar-bone with his left hand, in an undergrasp, and with his left leg forward. Uke grips tori, right side forward, and his right hand in an overgrasp.
Fig 32(b)   Typically, uke will be reluctant to

allow tori to grip with his right hand, so he tries to keep his left lapel and, in particular, his left sleeve out of tori's reach, while searching for the opportunity to get his own grip if tori makes a rash move.
Fig 32(c)   Tori closes the gap between them by shrugging his left shoulder under uke's stiff resisting right arm and bending his own arm, which has the effect of drawing them both closer together. Against a lighter man, tori would pull him forwards off-balance but, against a heavier man, who may be more difficult to move in this way, it is better to pull in to uke and perhaps cause him to bend forwards too.
Fig 32(d)   Sometimes it is necessary for tori to make a small step back on the right foot to cause uke to reach for tori's right sleeve. When uke does so, tori has the perfect opportunity to take his own grip.
Fig 32(e)   Generally, the most effective grip for this style of *osoto-gari* is at the biceps. The cloth there is usually loose enough to put the fingers straight in and get a grip on uke's sleeve that is very strong. It feels almost like a handle on his arm. This grip controls the elbow, rather than just the sleeve. By controlling uke's elbow, tori can transmit tension through uke's arm and shoulder and effectively control his whole upper body, enabling tori to then break his balance at the appropriate moment. It is important to notice their relative stances at this juncture. Tori has his left foot advanced, and uke has his left foot well back. Many opponents feel reasonably secure that they would be able to block any *osoto-gari* attempt if one were to be made in this situation. However, their sense of security is often illusory. At this stage tori has various options. For example, he could attack directly with *osoto-gari*.
Fig 32(f)   Alternatively, he could attempt to provoke a reaction in uke and first attack with *sasae-tsuri-komi-ashi*, blocking uke's right ankle with his left leg.
Fig 32(g)   The grip tori has with his right hand and on uke's elbow affords excellent control of uke, allowing tori to drive uke's left

(a)

(b)

(c)

(d)

(e)

(f)

(g)

(h)

(i)

(j)

(k)

(l)

(m)

arm up and push him off-balance over his forward leg. Frequently, this attack knocks uke down, sometimes he is thrown for ippon.

Fig 32(h)   If uke blocks the initial attack by pulling back and bracing against it, it gives tori a superb springboard effect to launch his *osoto-gari* with the same leg. Note the tension in uke's jacket as tori pulls himself in with both arms and drives the left hip through.

Fig 32(i)   Tori drives the leg past uke's rear leg and aims to contact with the back of his calf on the outside of his knee. The objective is to block his rear leg in such a way that he

cannot bend it. The foot should flick out like a boxer's fist when he throws a punch as the hands snatch uke into contact with tori's upper body.

Fig 32(j)   The perfect position for bringing off *osoto-gari*, Seisenbacher style. Uke is trapped with his weight pinned over his rear leg. Tori's right arm pulls uke's arm in tight to his body. Tori's left hand controls uke's head as he pushes against the side of his face. Once this position is reached, the chances of scoring ippon are excellent.

Fig 32(k)   The left arm pulls the right pushes.

The left leg switches from a principally blocking to a reaping action, hooking away uke's foundations as tori throws his body-weight into the technique.

Fig 32(l)   Tori's body bends at the waist and his head drives towards the floor as he reaps away uke's legs. Note how the hands complete the throw, steering and driving him flat onto his back.

Fig 32(m)   Ippon. The finishing position, at least, is nearly classical. Tori makes sure of the ippon by falling on top of uke, chest to chest. If the referee makes a mistake, tori has the advantage for *newaza*, providing he does not roll over him.

This ability to adapt is at the heart of the fundamental difference in approach between the traditional, conservative Japanese attitude and that of top western competitors. The Japanese will keep doing the same technique the same way in order to perfect it and, in their particular egoless form of practice, disregard the numerous times they are countered and the numerous attacks that fail against solid defences. There are many examples of Zen-based stories and sayings that embody this attitude such as, 'Fall down seven times, stand up eight', 'The forest is not so thick that from time to time a moonbeam cannot penetrate it', and 'By what I did yesterday, I win today, such is the virtue of practice'.

The western approach is inherently different and eclectic in a way the Japanese used to be. Western competitors adapt their techniques to their opponents, their approach makes them more able to analyse and modify. They change path easily and, true to the original tenets of judo, look for the path of least resistance, or at least the one that stands most chance of being effective. In a sense, the western attitude is slightly more cynical than that of the Japanese, who believe in the superiority of a rigidly defined ideal technique, so mechanically perfect that it will sooner or later prove effective whatever the circumstances. The westerner is more willing to adapt and compromise in order to win. Perhaps, the top Japanese competitors have the ability to adapt their technique too, but it is certainly more intuitive and less conscious than the western approach.

For the aspiring judo champion, this ability to change and develop is crucial to contest success in modern-day judo; one or two big guns are no longer sufficient. Technology has played a large part in developing this attitude among modern sports players. The advent of video, with slow motion, replay and freeze frame, means that there are no secrets anymore. Every successful attack and every mistake can be analysed and prepared for in the future. The sport has developed, the competitive nature of it makes it necessary that today's competitors be more adventurous, more adaptive and more willing to experiment and develop new skills than ever before. Such developments have to lead to increasingly higher standards among top competitors and the champions of the modern age must be stronger, fitter and more formidable than their predecessors, just as they are in all other sports. Of course, judoka will always argue about whether Yamashita at his best would have beaten Geesink or whether Parisi could have beaten Inokuma and so on, but such dream contests must remain just that.

3 The Modern View
by George Kerr and Peter Seisenbacher

THE PROFESSIONAL DEBATE

Judo is a system of physical and mental training of remarkable completeness, which was founded by Professor Jigoro Kano towards the end of the nineteenth century. As it was originally conceived, judo was much more than a mere sport, encompassing as it did a whole philosophy of training and discipline intended to provide trainees with an education for life. The original concept was that of *shugyo*, of an extremely severe self-imposed discipline, ascetic by modern standards, through which the trainee developed an iron-willed determination to succeed in whatever he put his mind to. Training was the way to forge the spirit and to develop mental power and intelligence, in order to deal with the problems of existence.

For the original judoka, judo was a way of life. The trainees studied, analysed and developed techniques but were never enslaved by the concept as many of today's young competitors seem to be. The rules were much less complicated and limiting; basically anything was allowed in *randori* (free play), as long as it was not calculated to injure one's training partners. Ultimately, the goal was not just to win on the mat, but self-realization, the creation of a person who could contribute something of value to the world.

Judo has evolved into a modern Olympic combat sport, something which traditionalists tend to see as having contributed to its deterioration. The pursuit of gold medals makes the sport a highly competitive, elitist activity and, at the highest level, there is only room for the most superb athletes. Many of these athletes now want to see professional rewards for their performance and dedication, inevitably comparing themselves to other sports players who seem to reap great financial profits from their talents.

The first major professional tournament took place in Paris after the Seoul Olympic games, and was dubbed 'The Prize-fight'. The original plan had been to re-introduce the idea of an open event, which was phased out of the Olympics, in order to encourage the unique possibility that has always traditionally existed in judo of smaller lighter men being able to take on and defeat bigger, heavier opponents. The four Olympic medallists in each weight category from under 78k to over 95k were invited to come and compete with the top four French fighters, all in one open tournament without weight categories. With over £30,000 in prize money being awarded to the successful contestants, the temptation was great but many nations declined the invitation and the event was an essentially European affair. The idea of professional judo tournaments may be in keeping with the spirit of the age, the zeitgeist of late twentieth-century capitalist society, but it is at odds with the original scope and breadth of Kano's vision, which had a much broader aim than solely material gratification. Notably absent from the tournament were the Japanese and Koreans.

The greatest objection to professionalism in judo is that it would sour the pure ethic of self-development that has always been at its root. There is also the fear that professionals would be at such a standard of fitness and combativity that they could no longer practise on equal terms with amateurs, which could kill judo as a recreational activity – in other words, judo as a sport for everyone.

These are issues that lie at the very root of judo as it continues to evolve into a modern, twentieth-century combat sport. For judo is not a fixed activity, with unchangeable rules or techniques. Like every modern sport, it must undergo changes in its rules from time to time to meet different needs in a changing world.

Tennis is one of a number of sports that has seen similar changes in recent decades. Initially, there was a strong reluctance on the part of its governing bodies to allow 'professionalism' into tennis. Those who broke the rules and toured a growing professional circuit were ostracized by the main body of ten-

nis players, or at least by the officials. However, now there is a more relaxed attitude towards professional tennis. The sport is able to cater for the needs of the professionals who, without doubt, are technically the most accomplished and capable players. In addition, there is an acknowledgement that the personalities, and even the antics, of some professionals act as a beacon – for good and evil – for a broadly based amateur sport. They are seen as entertainment for a passive audience as well as encouragement and inspiration for amateur players. Also some of the vast sums of money earned from the professional circuit benefits the grass roots.

Fig 33(a)–(c) Totikachvilli of the Soviet Union shows the all-action form that made him World Champion in 1989, with this superb drop knee *kata-guruma* against the Austrian, Hipsmeier.

Fig 33 (a) Totikachvilli makes a close range attack, initially with a fairly orthodox attempt at *kata-guruma* which his Austrian opponent attempts to counter with *ko-uchi-gari*.

Fig 33 (b)   Totikachvilli disengages his right leg and drops to his left knee, tipping Hipsmeier over his head.

Fig 33 (c)   Totikachvilli adds impetus to the technique by driving with the legs and thrusting with the right arm as he pulls with the left, to dump his opponent on his back.

Unfortunately, a direct comparison with judo cannot be drawn. Although judo is, at least in the West, seen as a combat sport, even the man in the street cannot totally equate it with winning and losing, cups and medals. Curiously, perhaps, part of its popular appeal is that it represents a more unsullied ethic. Most players in the dojos would not use the word *shugyo*, but most recognize a feeling that judo can make new men and women of them, and that throwing a particular opponent or winning a particular medal is only part of the story.

Allowing judo players to become professionals would seem to cause other difficulties. In most countries, judo is what is termed a minority sport with relatively small numbers. Yet, unlike athletics, for example, or even tennis, many training partners are needed to develop the complex skills. Where would the professionals find their training partners? Surely, if they practised in amateur clubs they would decimate the memberships within months.

On closer investigation, this problem is already being encountered. International judo fighters are already professional in all but name; most are training full-time. Generally, they learn to adapt the level of *randori* training to their partners. If they are with an older partner or *kyu* grade, they handicap themselves and take care in the use of their strongest techniques. Only if they are practising with other young contest fighters do they go all out. Many of these modern sportsmen and women cannot see why they should not be able to earn a living from their sport as their colleagues in tennis or cricket. They argue that the old days, when it was expected to devote oneself to such an activity for the love of it, have gone. It is worth noting that great champions such as Anton Geesink and Shota Chochoshvilli became professional wrestlers in Japan (earning the condemnation of the judo movement) because, they argued, they had no other means of earning a living.

So many of the current judo champions

welcome the money tournments and the introduction of other methods to attract a television audience, such as the blue and white judogi adopted by the European Judo Union. It is significant that virtually every major rule development that has taken place in judo, from weight categories to passivity rulings, have been initiated in the West.

These modern views are objected to virulently by those who hold more traditional views, and they are by no means just the older judoka. Part of their concern is that, instead of a vigorous world judo movement with millions of practitioners and a few hundred champions, there might be only a few hundred professionals who perform for pay and whose function is to entertain a passive audience, as is the case with professional boxing. However, there are others who argue that true professionalism is the only way to ensure equal competition, since all competitors would then be on equal terms. A healthy amateur movement could thrive alongside. Therefore, the arguments are complex.

RECREATIONAL JUDO: EDUCATION THROUGH LEISURE

The other side of the coin to professional sport in western culture is the amateur approach and, given that only an elite few can ever make it to the highest levels, it is in the amateur arena where the greatest potential for the expansion of judo lies. Judo can be practised, studied and enjoyed on many different levels and it is important for the future of judo that governing bodies and individual clubs recognize this and respond accordingly. For the activity to thrive, it has to cater for the youngsters who are, as in all aspects of life, the future. There has to be provision for the ambitious, highly motivated competitor, perhaps training full-time and looking for success at national and international level, but also for the older player who simply wants to go to the club and have a pull-around and some exercise.

There will always be those who seek self-development and education through judo, but, increasingly, in the West the coach or instructor has replaced the teacher. Real judo teachers in the classical sense are now hard to find. There are many modern clubs where the emphasis is on technical instruction and many instructors who can teach to a reasonably high level of competence in the physical aspects of the sort of judo, but the *do* or 'way' that Kano postulated is in little evidence. However, there remains some scope for a westernization of the notion of *do*, which would ultimately benefit the practitioners of judo and the activity itself. It can be a superb vehicle for developing self-discipline and for teaching the value of correct behaviour and courtesy.

The Japanese flavour, which judo has always had, is something that needs to be retained. Most people accept the need for discipline and regard the basic manners of judo, the etiquette and the courtesy as important as ever. For a long time, western adherents of judo had an ongoing love affair with things Japanese, but it must be admitted that, of late, there has been a change in attitude. Some no longer have the same enthusiasm for traditional Japanese values. This is not just happening in the West. Recently, Nobuyuki Sato, one of Japan's foremost judo teachers, made a speech about the future of judo in Japan at Busen Mondai Gyakku University, a place famous for producing judo men in the samurai tradition. Speaking on the nature of judo and on the theme of the preservation of tradition he made a very interesting observation saying, 'Why should the Japanese child do judo when he can play baseball?' The level of appeal has to be more than simple hedonism. Doing judo for fun is fine, but a youngster might equally well play football, or indeed baseball, if the only motivation is play or enjoyment.

Judo has many different and compatible levels of appeal, particularly for the non-Japanese. As well as the obvious physical benefits of sport, fitness and self-defence, there are mental and cultural benefits. The judo student develops discipline, fighting spirit, correct attitude and control, as well as learning something of the Japanese language and culture, which often stimulates further study not confined to just judo. There is also the kinaesthetic element, the awareness and enjoyment of movement, and the social interaction that occurs whenever people with similar interests get together.

There will always be changes and we have to adapt to them and live with them, but some things are worth preserving. For judo to retain its uniqueness, the Japanese flavour has to be retained because its traditions are Japanese. As an analogy, golf is a Scottish sport, the first ever game being played on Leith Links and the traditions have endured. Credit should be given where it is due; the originators of the sport deserve some recognition, whenever it is played.

The newcomer to judo is likely to find himself practising in a club where the emphasis is on training for competition, simply because that is what most people enjoy most, the *randori*, trying to throw a resisting opponent who is trying to throw you. There is nothing wrong with this and, of course, the more people enjoy what they are doing the more likely it is that they will carry on doing it. This is essentially healthy and is the grass roots, even the life-blood, of the judo movement in the West. However, it is a bit like reducing a game of football to a penalty-taking contest. The future of judo does not lie purely in the enjoyment of the sport, whether as participant or spectator, but in education through the sport.

Once the competitor's day is done, there is a whole world of experiences awaiting those who wish to continue to practise and try to achieve things within judo. The range of possibilities is huge, from the micro-environment where the extent of a person's ambition might be to become a referee or a teacher to the macro or global level where policy can be developed within a national association and promoted through the IJF, in order that change within judo can be directed and channelled in a controlled way for the maximum possible benefit.

JUDO AS PHYSICAL TRAINING

People who have never done judo can be forgiven for not realizing how physically demanding it is. The good fighters make it look incredibly easy and the bad ones, beginners usually, just look hopelessly unfit. The general public probably only realized there was anything phyically demanding about the sport with the advent of the English TV programme, *Superstars*, which saw Brian Jacks demonstrate the remarkable combination of athletic abilities that had kept him at the top in judo for so long, to become European Superstars Champion, beating top sportsmen from a variety of other activities in the process.

The judo player needs to be strong, agile, quick and possess good endurance powers. One of the reasons judo is such a demanding sport is that fighters suffer from restricted oxygen intake as a result of being bent over and unable to breathe freely for large parts of the training and contest. The relativley fit person, new to judo, pretty soon becomes aware of the deficiencies in his forearms, lower back and neck as a result of gripping and being pulled around. In the case of the novice who has done no other type of sport or foundation training, every muscle in the body seems to suffer and many complain of chronic muscle stiffness for days after the first session. Many clubs run beginners courses for just this reason, to prepare the novice for his first 'real' session.

The beginner invariably discovers that the first problem is grip strength. The forearms pump up and it becomes impossible to move the fingers after a few minutes of maximum effort in a grading or *kyu* grade competition. This is due to the build-up of lactic acid in the muscles. Regular training in either the strength endurance circuit using weights or the specialist grip exercises described in Chapter 5 take care of this.

Perhaps more than in any other sport, the judo player needs a complete balance of physical qualities and must develop his speed, strength, skill, stamina and suppleness, in harmony. There have been many extremely impressive judo champions who were renowned for their excellent fitness at all weights, including Katsuhiko Kashiwazaki, Robert van de Walle, Dietmar Lorenz and Neil Adams. All of these champions at their peak were incredibly fit and a match for just about any top sportsman in the world. Training methods and preferences among the top fighters differ considerably but all demand extremely hard work.

Among judo players, the lighter-weight category fighters tend to have the most efficient builds, and the nature of lightweight judo calls for the ability to work at a very high energy output continuously throughout a contest. Lightweight action tends to be non-stop and, pound for pound, these fighters are among the fittest and strongest of athletes. Conversely, the heavyweights tend not to be so fit. There are exceptions of course: Anton Geesink and Wilhelm Ruska were veritable giants and Yasuhiro Yamashita, despite a deceptive roundness to his physique, was always in top condition for contest.

WOMEN'S JUDO

One of the most significant developments in judo over the past twenty years has been the introduction of international competition for women, which is very much a western innovation. Although women have practised in both the East and West for decades, the attitudes were very differnt. In Britain in the 1950s, as in many European countries, women were a normal feature of dojo life. In Japan, at the same time, there were women doing judo, but mainly in separate dojos – and the emphasis was on *kata* as much as *randori*. However, there were no competitions for women. The egalitarian western approach did much to open up sports opportunities in judo for women, with a greater awareness of technical needs and differences as a result.

In the West, women tended to be taught the same techniques in the same manner as men, ignoring the fact that their physical abilities and mental attitudes are often different. Women do not have the same natural level of explosive power, upper body strength or speed of men and, therefore, their judo has to be more technically based. On the other hand, they seem to have a higher pain barrier, and even higher endurance. (It is interesting to note that there are far fewer passivity warnings in women's judo than in men's judo).

Nevertheless, there was and there remains a noticeably condescending attitude – and even mysogyny – from many men in judo towards women on the mat. This is particularly the case in Japan where judo was not readily seen

Fig 34   Superb technical control from Britain's four-times world bantamweight champion, Karen Briggs, as she throws Lyn Porier (Canada) for ippon with *tai-otoshi* in the Commonwealth Games in Edinburgh, 1986.

Fig 35 Ingrid Berghmans, the most successful competitor in women's judo to date, with world and European titles in both her light heavyweight category and the open, holding down Hakansson (Sweden) in the 1986 World Championships in Maastricht.

Fig 36 Fumiko Esaki, Japan's world bantamweight silver medallist, throwing Cho (Korea) with a fine *kouchi-gari-makikomi* in the Olympic demonstration tournament in Seoul in 1988.

Fig 37 Well-controlled *ashiwaza* from Shigemoto (USA) against Ruth Vondy (Britain) in the light heavyweight category of the 1983 British Open.

Fig 38   A spirited *uchimata-makikomi* by Mochida (Japan) in the Seoul Olympics. Her opponent had started to counter the *uchimata* with a pick–up, but was lifted cleanly into the air with the *makikomi*.

as a fit activity for the feminine sex. In the early years of international women's competition, for a Japanese teacher to be appointed a women's coach was akin to being sent to Siberia. By the 1980s, as the entry of women's judo to the Olympics only became a matter of time, this attitude changed, and now women are generally accepted in judo in much the same way as they are in athletics or swimming.

It must also be noted that, as a result of a proper competition structure for women, the general technical level of women's judo has improved. Champions such as Karen Briggs from Great Britian, Ingrid Berghmans from Belgium and Edith Hrovath from Austria

Fig 39   Loretta Doyle, Britain's 1982 world featherweight champion, attacks with *ouchi-gari* at the World Championships in Vienna, 1984.

(a)

(b)

Fig 40 (a) and (b)   A good example of feminine flexibility. Tracy Lee has won the dominant grip over Jackie Johnson in the British trials (1987) and with good rotation throws her cleanly for ippon.

74

(known particularly for her *newaza*), demonstrated excellent accomplishment and good fighting spirit. They have been among the most consistently successful competitors of the 1980s. There has also been a similar increase in fitness as women acknowledged the demands of modern competition judo and adopted carefully prepared weights and fitness programmes. Apart from exceptional individuals such as Kaori Yamaguchi, Japanese success came more slowly in women's judo, but it has been making more of an impact recently.

The final acceptance of women's judo in the 1992 Olympics will bring the public face of the sport into line with what is happening in dojos throughout the world.

JUDO EAST AND WEST: SOME SIMILARITIES AND DIFFERENCES

A major difference between judo in the East and West is the sprung floor that is common to all Japanese dojos and is generally purpose-built for judo. There are very few of these in the West. The effect of the sprung floor is to encourage movement and spring to allow the judoka to train with less fear of injury, and to move faster and without inhibition. Therefore, it is a great aid to acquiring feeling and balance in judo. The typical western judo club mat is slower than the Japanese surface and, because taking falls is harder, players tend to be more defensive and attempt to pin their opponents in place, rather than risking moving with them.

This major physical difference in the type of dojo training surface leads to other differences in style and emphasis. The Japanese attitude to being thrown is more relaxed; *randori* should be adventurous, so being caught is relatively unimportant (although competition, of course, is a different matter). In the West, on the other hand, there is a lot of ego involved in practice. People do not want to be thrown and take great pains to avoid it. Besides it can be painful on a hard surface. The tendency then is for western judo to be stiffer, less mobile and more defensive, although obviously this is a generalization and there are many exceptions. Dojos in the West also tend to be smaller than in Japan and have smaller mat areas, consequently there is less space and room to move which further influences the style of the judo.

In terms of general skill level, there is still a considerable difference in ability. Gripping is an area where the Japanese are noticeably superior. Only our very best fighters can match their skill levels in that area. Many westerners, when they first train in Japan, are shocked by how inferior their gripping is compared with even average players. They all have to make a special effort to remedy the situation. It is evident that we, in the West, still do not grip properly a lot of the time.

The other big area of difference between the Japanese and the West is that the traditional Japanese teaching method accepts that judo takes a long time to learn correctly. Proper attention is given to *tai-sabaki* (body movement), *tsukuri* (balance breaking) and *kake* (execution and finishing). Despite success in international competitions, technical competence in the West tends to be more superficial than in Japan. There is too much rushing to get the hang of too many different techniques.

CONCLUSIONS

The modern approach needs to be eclectic. We must keep what is good from the old yet take advantage of worthwhile developments that occur. For example, there is no reason why traditional Japanese etiquette, such as the formal bow, should not be retained. It both introduces and emphasizes a level of courtesy that contributes to the special atmosphere of a dojo. Similarly, while the names of the techniques can be taught in the

Fig 41(a) Competition is often a question of compromise, making the best of a given situation. This happens even when East meets West, as here. Competitor No. 523 has attacked with *osoto-gari*, but using an *ippon-seoi-nage* grip. It is a mixed attack that has a reasonable technical base and is seen relatively frequently but its main strength is the surprise factor.

Fig 41(b) However, his Japanese opponent has not been caught napping. He has stopped the attack, and now begins to turn to take over control, aiding the counter-attack by pulling on the belt. 523 cannot prevent the turn because he has no control of his opponent's right-hand side of the body, which is the main weakness of the grip.

Fig 41(c) The flexibility and willingness to attempt a counter has worked. The Japanese has turned well and, even though he has lost his grip on the belt, all the weight of 523 is now on his heel. Therefore, he is badly off balance, even though the Japanese is only gripping with one hand.

Fig 41(d) 523 cannot prevent the throw, and now has to twist as much as he can to lessen the score.

Fig 42 Not much flexibility here, but there is power and position to compensate. Jean-Michel Berthet gives a typical example of strong western judo style. His grip, which is fairly traditional, has completely dominated his opponent, but his entry has come from a surge of power. Once past the leg, he clamps his opponent to him and drops to a knee to make sure there is no escape. His opponent must have felt he was pole-axed.

Fig 43 However, western judo can produce some eminently smooth stylists too. Here, in his bronze medal fight at the World Championships in Essen, Seisenbacher's old rival, Densign White, footsweeps Gheorgi Petrov (Bulgaria) with an elegant *de-ashi-barai* for ippon. Not much strength here, just a straightforward grip, direct movement – and a sixth sense for the perfect timing.

Fig 44(a)–(c)   Koga of Japan attacks Majemite of Nigeria with an unconventional one-handed *sode-tsuri-komi-goshi* in the 1989 World Championships.

Fig 44(a)   Koga turns in for a mongrel *sode-tsuri*, over-rotating by conventional standards, but the depth of his attack, the speed and the hip height are enough to upend his opponent. He catches the Nigerian's leg with his free left arm to prevent him avoiding the technique in the way that he would like.

Fig 44(b)   The good points of this attack are apparent; Koga dips his head well and drives powerfully with his legs, but he has no real control of Majemite and the Nigerian is able to put out his free right hand to avoid being thrown by doing a kind of one-handed handstand.

Fig 44(c)   Koga reacts by trying to roll and finish the technique, but Majemite is able to twist out and avoid conceding the ippon. A spectacular attack, though, of the kind that, even when unsuccessful, catches the judges' eye.

Fig 45(a)–(d) Toshihiko Koga of Japan throws Chang Su Lee of Korea with one of the most spectacular and talked about throws in modern judo, which demonstrated how a classical technique can be transformed. At the moment when he made this attack, Koga was holding with just his right hand, but a great debate has grown up as to whether he actually did the throw one-handed or caught hold of some part of the Korean's judogi with his left hand as he completed. Even though the event was televised, the camera angles made it impossible to say with any certainty what he did with his left hand.

Fig 45(a) Koga's style of *seoi-nage* relies on very fast footwork, running under his opponents and exploding underneath them. In this case, he drives the right hip in deep as he pulls his opponent over his back.

Fig 45(b) Koga changes the distribution of his weight from the left foot to the right even after he has begun to lift his opponent, in order to get the left leg still further underneath the Korean to maximize hip turn and lift.

Fig 45(c) The spring in the legs and particularly the drive from the left leg is obvious as Koga hurls his opponent to the mat.

Fig 45(d) The total commitment to finishing the technique is evidenced by the way Koga throws himself on top of his opponent.

language of the country, it is both of educational and social benefit to maintain the Japanese names for them as well. It is one of the particular pleasures of judo to be able to arrive in a foreign country and join a practice even if you are unable to speak the language of the country. After all, you will all speak a smattering of Japanese.

It is important for this awareness of courtesy to extend to general behaviour on the mat. Everyone has special needs: the competito r needs to be tested, the *kyu* grade needs to be allowed to develop his techniques, the older person needs to enjoy his judo session without feeling that his body can no longr take the strain. With imagination, everyone can get something from a practice, no matter how different the standards. This is where the professional and amateur, the young and old, meet, and there is no likelihood that general judo practice in the West will change in this respect.

If such courtesy is not maintained and the needs of competition prevail, judo will suffer and decline, as has happened in other western combat sports. This does not just mean that the competition judoka must take care with the recreational judoka in *randori*. It also involves maintaining the other judo activities such as *kata*. Working on *nage-no-kata* or *ju-no-kata* may not appeal to a young blood with medals in mind, but, in fact, it probably would not do him or her any harm and things can be learnt from a *kata* that can be put to good use in a modern contest. Apart from that, *kata* developed to a high standard is an absorbing aesthetic experience for the practitioners, and even for an audience.

It is also worth remembering that the prevailing popular public image of judo remains that of a self-defence system in which the small person can defeat a larger aggressor. If the modern judo club wishes to thrive, it needs to recognize this potential market and cater for it, rather than simply allow *ju-jitsu* and the punching/kicking systems to dominate. Interestingly, this is an area which is as undeveloped in Japan as it is in the West: judo for self-defence is rarely taught or practised in the home of judo, other than in occasional conventional *kata* forms.

It is important not to dismiss new ideas which clearly have a usefulness. The video camera and the facility it offers for instant recording and playback is a great boon to both coach and competitor, and even to the recreational player intent on improving a technique. It allows them to study and analyse an opponent's techniques, strengths and weaknesses, and observe the mistakes that they themselves make, both in the heat of contest and in training.

It is also useful to study videos of the top competitions. After all, competition is the cutting edge of judo in a technical sense. It is at the World Championships, the Olympic games and other top internationals that new techniques are introduced. Sometimes, it appears that they are simply new versions of older ones, temporarily forgotten. However, there is no doubt that one of the advantages of competition is that they prevent judo from becoming fossilized.

Judo is still evolving and, in some ways, that is its strength. We have come a long way from Jigoro Kano and his eight-tatami dojo in Eishoji Temple. It offers many things to many people and, despite the physical and mental demands it makes upon its adherents, often attracts a lifetime's commitment. George Kerr's judo life appears very different to Peter Seisenbacher's judo life, and so they are, yet both can be characterized by one word: fulfilment.

4 Contest Judo:
Championship Winning Techniques
by Peter Seisenbacher

Modern judo is principally a dynamic and demanding combat sport comprising two main areas: *tachiwaza* or standing techniques and *newaza* or ground fighting. Both areas place quite different demands on the individual and considerable training in both departments is absolutely essential in order to make real progress.

Developing strong *newaza* is generally felt to be less problematic than acquiring good standing techniques, as the former requires rather less natural talent and those intangible qualities of feeling and confidence that are so much more difficult to teach than the mechanics of mere technique. *Newaza* is slower and anyone willing to work hard can make progress, even older people who come to judo quite late.

Excellence in *tachiwaza* tends to be the domain of people who begin judo when they are young children or teenagers and who carry on training for many years. This is not just for physical reasons, but because the young mind is more flexible and adaptive and able to respond to new ideas more rapidly. Physical factors do play a large part, of course, and it is noticeable that physical priorities differ according to weight category. The speed of neuro-muscular coordination and motor reflexes begins to deteriorate in the early twenties, hence the majority of fighters in the lightweight category, where work-rate, fitness and speed tend to be the deciding factors are usually in their early or mid-twenties. Among the heavyweights, strength and durability are more important, and the bigger men and women generally manage to have longer careers. Even so, the best heavyweights are fast and tend to be at their peak in their mid- to late twenties.

The younger a person is when they begin doing judo, the longer they have to acquire and develop skill, as long as they are carefully nurtured and looked after. I began doing judo at the age of eight, as did Neil Adams. Yamashita began at the age of ten, but some begin considerably later and achieved similar success, Angelo Parisi was fourteen and David Starbrook was nineteen, so there are no hard and fast rules about how old you must be to become a champion. The common elements are desire, determination and dedication. The judo player who simply enjoys the activity and is not concerned with becoming a World or Olympic Champion need not worry his or herself with statistics. Their time can be better spent practising. (It is interesting to note how many successful champions also enjoyed other sports at an early age, champions as varied as Nobuyuki Sato, Neil Adams and even Karen Briggs all played football to quite a high junior standard before deciding to concentrate on judo.) One thing they have in common with would-be champions, though, is that they must find out what techniques can work for them and try to incorporate them in their repertoire. However, before embarking upon any analysis of specific needs and strategies, it is advisable to have a general understanding of what the judo situation involves. The standard confrontation between two opponents, that is *tachiwaza*, whether it be contest, *kata* or *randori*, is the heart of judo.

CONTEST (SHIAI)

To the uninitiated, contest seems to be the most easily understood, being essentially a wrestling match between two athletes. The non-judoka rarely grasps just how extremely arduous it is, little guessing the amount of psychological and physical energy that gets burned up in the course of a tournament. In the last twenty years, contest has changed out of all recognition from what it was. The chief reason for this has been the development of the notion of contest as sport. Thirty years ago, if two men stepped on the mat to do judo they would tend to allow one another to take their preferred grips by tacit mutual consent and then proceed to stalk around the mat waiting for a mistake to happen, perhaps very occasionally trying to precipitate one. Often the most obvious sign of activity was the perspiration on the participants' foreheads as they probed one another's defences with the occasional *ashiwaza*. When an attack did come, it would usually be decisive or would be equally decisively countered. The contest was entirely between the fighters, it was not intended to be a spectator sport for audience entertainment.

The inclusion of judo in the Olympics in 1964 was the first step towards changing this utterly. The parallel development of the media, particularly televison which in the modern day covers every imaginable activity, had a profound influence on the judo contest. Spectator interest became a priority and changes to the rule structure of the sport were implemented with the intention of making it more attractive to spectators, particularly those with little or no prior knowledge of judo.

When one person acts, so another allows himself to be acted upon, or reacts, and it is in this interplay between individuals that the interest of judo lies. Attack and defence are the principles upon which judo is founded, embodying the principles of the active and the passive, action and reaction all within the context of a physical and psychological challenge concluding in success or failure. The whole process is designed to be self-testing and to encourage self-development in order to be equal to the test.

RANDORI

Randori, or free practice, is the proving ground for contest-effective techniques. Players practise in a less pressurized way than they would if they were fighting in tournament, although it is quite intense on occasion within the practice. *Randori* can easily degenerate into a sort of contest with no referees or prizes, with one player solely interested in defeating the other, but this is a very poor kind of *randori*. The aim of free practice should be to learn and to experiment. It is necessary to take risks and change things in order to make progress. Weaknesses can be worked on constructively and strengths developed. It is one of the few times when winning and losing are not really considerations and the judoka ought to be able to forget about ego and simply participate wholeheartedly in the activity.

KATA

Kata embodies the forms of judo technique and the principles for the rational use of force. Its study is certainly not essential to contest effectiveness, but its discipline offers something different and equally of value to the student. Currently the practice of *kata* is not popular. It tends to be regarded as a boring and outmoded form of training and consequently standards are generally low. This is a situation that has come about as a result of judging everything from the point of view of contest effectiveness. *Kata* is an activity which need not be performance related, but which provides balanced and beneficial exercise for the whole body is performed regularly. Its usefulness and its meaning have never been successfully communicated and until they are its practice seems likely to remain sporadic and undeveloped. This is a remarkable contrast to the situation that exists in martial arts, such as karate and taekwondo, where the *kata* are seen to be reservoirs of learning and knowledge and training in them is felt to be at least as important as contest ability.

MA-AI: THE FOUR AREAS

Whatever the judo situation, whether it be contest, *kata* or *randori*, an extremely important element is that of distance. Traditionally, the Japanese martial arts made specialized studies of calculating distance, known as *ma-ai*. This is relevant within the context of judo, particularly contest. There are four situations that can be identified where there is a potential for an attack, which are characterized by the distances separating the fighters and subseqently by the grips the fighters take.

The No-Grip Situation

The first situation is that which immediately follows the command *hajime* at the beginning of a contest or at any time after matte (break) has been called. This is the situation where two fighters confront one another but neither has yet taken a hold. An attacking opportunity exists for one or the other to rush in and immediately attempt to throw the opponent before they have time to react. Certain simple techniques lend themselves well to this situation, usually they involve rushing the opponent, then grabbing his legs to trip him or picking him up and throwing him to his rear, as with *morote-gari*.

Robert van de Walle of Belgium was a master of this technique and could produce a decisive *morote-gari* at any point in a contest. Ben Spykers of Holland is renowned for the success he has with the same technique, frequently deciding close contests in the dying seconds by springing this technique which always seems to take his opponents by surprise, even though they must be expecting it because he always does it!

Opening Gambits *(Fig 47(a)–(c))*
These two attacks are just two among many possible scoring techniques often used in contest before the opponent has even taken his grip (*see* page 46).

Fig 47(a) The moment when contest begins, just prior to either fighter taking a grip. The danger starts here!

Fig 47(b) *Morote-gari* is a common but often effective attack. Tori simply bends and grabs both uke's legs behind the knees then lifts and drives with the legs (*see* the superb contest example of Azcuy of Cuba on Maselli of Italy (Fig 46).

Fig 47(c) One hand grips high and pushes to the rear as the other grabs behind the knee, blocking any attempt to recover balance and allowing tori to push his surprised opponent to the mat.

The One-Handed Grip

The second level of contact occurs when one of the fighters has one hand on his opponent. This seemingly minimal contact can be a dangerous situation, especially against *ippon-seoi-nage* specialists or fighters skilled in *ashi-iwaza*. Usually, this kind of technique requires an element of surprise or a large skill gap between the fighters in order to be successful. The high incidence of contests won by *seoi-nage* indicates that it is potentially a very good situation from which to score. Often the opponent does not feel so threatened by a one-handed grip as he would by a two-handed approach and so is lulled into a false sense of security and concedes the score. Again attacks to the rear are a real possibility since the free hand can be used to grab a leg or to push unexpectedly. This grip allows numerous possibilities for sudden attack; e.g. *ude-gaeshi* and *ippon-seoi-nage*.

Fig 46(a)–(d)   A superb example of *morote-gari* by the Cuban, Isaac Azcuy, against Maselli of Italy from the Tournoi de Paris in 1982.

Fig 46(a)   The Cuban runs in under his opponent's guard and scoops both legs up, catching the Italian behind the knees whilst driving his shoulder up into Maselli's armpit to heave him off-balance. The Italian, instead of letting go and spinning out onto his front, tries to defend by grabbing Azcuy's right trouser leg with his left hand – a bad mistake in this case.

Fig 46(b)   Azcuy continues his drive, pulling Maselli's right leg up high with his left hand while twisting to his left to completely turn the Italian's hips, and dives for the mat.

Fig 46(c)   The turning action of the right hand is crucially important to the success of this technique and is clearly visible in this picture as the Italian's back lands flat on the ground.

Fig 46(d)   Note how Azcuy has instinctively released his left hand in order to prevent Maselli from rolling him over in *newaza*, should the ippon not have been awarded.

Fig 47(a)

Fig 47(b)

Fig 47(c)

(a)

(b)

(c)

(d)

(e)

Fig 48(a)–(e)   Finding the path of least resistance. This fascinating sequence shows the awesome skill, agility and power of one of the greatest western judoka, Angelo Parisi of England and France.

Fig 48(a)   Parisi leaps into the attack with left *osoto-gari*. This attack had been preceded by a similarly committed right *osoto-gari* attack which the Russian Chochoshvilli, who was holding left, defended by withdrawing his left leg and twisting his upper body to the right. This created the perfect opportunity for the extremely supple Parisi to come in on the other side, holding as usual with his unorthodox double lapel grip. The Russian is completely wrong-footed, his powerful arms bypassed.

Fig 48(b)   A splendid picture of commitment and poise. Chochoshvilli defends desperately by throwing back his right leg, but he is very well controlled by Parisi who, having created the opportunity, exploits it to the full.
Fig 48(c)   The direction of the throw changes as Parisi accommodates Chochoshvilli's attempt to defend. The powerful rotation of the body, the continuous pulling action of the hands and dynamic reaping action of the left leg combine to make an unstoppable ippon.
Fig 48(d)   Chochoshvilli is thrown for ippon, flat on his back.
Fig 48(e)   There is no doubt as to the victor or the vanquished!

Kuchiki-Taoshi *Fig 49(a)–(c)*
This sequence shows a variation of *tani-otoshi*, sometimes called *kuchiki-taoshi* or 'Dead Tree Drop'.

Fig 49(a)   This situation is known as *kenka yotsu*: Tori is in a left fighting stance and uke is standing, right-handed. He is griping tori's left lapel with his hand and tori holds uke's right lapel with his left hand.

Fig 49(b)   Tori shrugs with his shoulder and steps inside past uke's stiff right arm, placing his left foot behind uke's forward leg as he pulls down on uke's right lapel with his left hand.

Fig 49(c)   Tori reaches down with his free right hand and grabs for uke's leg behind the knee and pulls it up as he pulls uke's upper body downwards, wheeling him to the mat. If uke tries to step back, it is sometimes necessary to catch the leg at the ankle. It is also possible to lunge and sit down as you push and reap away his back leg with your advanced left leg. This is especially effective if uke tries to hop back on his left foot.

(a)

(b)

(c)

The Classic Two-Handed Grip

There are many different ways that a contest can be fought but, to many judoka, the orthodox approach where both fighters grip up with two hands and set about trying to throw one another for ippon, with the traditional classical techniques of the Gokyo, is the most appealing. The aesthetic element of the appeal of sport judo is particularly well satisfied by a scything foot-sweep, a blindingly fast *tai-otoshi* or an unstoppable *harai-goshi*. For many people, myself included, the judo which comes about as a result of fighting and practising in this way is the best. It is at once the most skilful and the most difficult to perform, but the most satisfying to see and to experience. The contact and control afforded by the two-handed grip, where both players are at arms length from one another, is good and allows for considerable freedom of movment on the part of both players. To bring off a throw, ground has to be covered and risks must be taken. The possibilities for combination techniques are boundless as well.

Fig 50   Koga, the Japanese lightweight champion, who was a surprise failure at the Seoul Olympics, although he did win the world title in Belgrade in 1989. A *seoi-nage* specialist, his classical gripping did not prove effective against the canny Tenadze of the Soviet Union.

Fig 51(a)–(d) A superb right *morote-seoi-nage* by the incomparable Angelo Parisi on Clemens Jehle of Switzerland.

Fig 51(a) Using the unorthodox double lapel grip, Parisi turns under his much bigger opponent. The positioning of the hips is perfect; Parisi's lower back is below Jehle's centre of gravity and forms a fulcrum over which he can pull him with his hands and the forward bending action of his body. Note the relative heights of both men's belts.

Fig 51(b) A perfect throwing action. The legs drive powerfully as the upper body rotates and the hands completely control Jehle's upper body. The left hand makes a smooth continuous pull as the right pins and guides. The length of the right forearm is in contact with Jehle's chest.

Fig 51(c) Pull turns to push as Parisi finishes the throw very aggressively, planting Jehle flat on his back with a straightening of the arms and the full commitment of his body-weight.

Fig 51(d) The circular nature of the throwing action and the abandonment necessary for such spectacular success are apparent in the final frame of the throw.

The Two-Handed Classical Grip *Fig 51(a)–(c)*

This grip allows for the greatest possible range of throwing techniques.
Fig 52(a)   They both hold, left-handed in this instance.

Fig 52(b)   Attacks to the rear with techniques such as *kouchi-gari* are possible.

Fig 52(c) Forward attacks with techniques such as *tai-otoshi* are typical from this grip.

The Grappling-Style Approach

This fourth stage of contact is much favoured by Soviet fighters, probably as a result of their traditions in Sombo wrestling. It involves getting the most possible amount of body contact, closing right in on an opponent and putting him under severe pressure to make a mistake. Aesthetically, it is certainly not so appealing as the traditional style, but there is no denying its effectiveness if you allow this style of fighter to dominate the gripping. It is particularly favoured by taller fighters, especially those with long arms as they can reach right over the top of an opponent's shoulders and down his back to grab the belt. The 1989 World Light/Heavyweight Champion, Koba Kurtanidze of the Soviet Union, is one of the most effective exponents of this approach to judo. The 1990 European Champion, Stephane Traineau of France, is another. Such men are devastatingly effective once they can reach over the top and get hold of their opponent's belt, as they can generate enormous power to bring off spectacular hip techniques such as *tsuri-goshi* and *harai-goshi*. This style of judo lacks subtlety though, relying on great physical power in the upper body to dominate the opponent by crushing his defence and then blasting through with the power of the legs. Such fighters tend not to have a very great range of throwing skills, relying instead on their big guns to win the day.

The grip makes the judo they plan to do predictable, but if they win the battle for grips, quite often they have won the contest. Allowing this kind of fighter to take their favoured grip is tantamount to suicide.

Grappling *Fig 53(a)–(d)*
The closest style of fighting, as favoured by Russian judoka, is less pretty than traditional judo but undeniably dangerous.
Fig 53(a)   The unorthodox over-the-shoulder grip, pulling uke in and keeping him bent over.
Fig 53(b)   As well as major hip throws, it is common for fighters employing this grip to attack with *ouchi-gari*.
Fig 53(c)   Uke has to anticipate the unconventional when facing such forms of attack. *Ouchi-gari* can be followed by a leg grab to pin the opponent.
Fig 53(d)   Tori may even then switch outside to a *kosoto-gari* or *sukui-nage* type of attack. It is very dangerous to give anyone this degree of contact as it is easy to get thrown by letting an opponent in so close.

It is a curious fact that this grappling style of judo is something that came back into fashion with the advent of Russian judoka on the international scene yet the same techniques can be found in the repertoire of the old ju jitsu schools, where combat effectiveness was the governing criteria for study or use.

(a)

(b)

(c)

(d)

Kumikata: Gripping Techniques

The grip is the key to effective *tachiwaza* and all judoka have their preferred methods of gripping in order to bring off their favourite techniques. I am naturally a left-handed fighter but the majority of my opponents were right-handed so I evolved my own particular method of getting my grip which was generally very effective. This sequence shows the logical procedure I evolved to get my favourite grip which allowed me to attack with a variety of major throws such as *osoto-gari*, *ouchi-gari* and as in this example, *uchimata*.

An Effective Grip *Fig 54(a)–(m)*

Fig 54(a)   Tori allows uke to grip his left lapel with his right hand.

Fig 54(b)   Tori lifts his left arm so that his forearm pushes against uke's, which has the effect of slightly bending his arm at the elbow, thereby opening up his defence.

Fig 54(c)   In a flash, tori drives his arm inside uke's reaching for the collar of his jacket behind his neck.

(a)

(b)

(c)

95

Fig 54(d) Tori grabs uke's judogi at the neck and pulls down on uke's head, his left arm continuing to grip inside uke's right.

Fig 54(e) Tori then reaches for uke's sleeve and inserts his fingers into the cloth at the elbow.

Fig 54(f)   Tori has achieved his aim and from this grip can throw his opponent with a number of techniques. The control tori has is very strong and uke is held in an unnatural bent-over position, which makes him uncomfortable.

Fig 54(g)   When tori feels uke resist his downward pressure and attempts to straighten up, tori quickly relaxes the tension, allowing him to do so.

Fig 54(h) This is the moment that tori chooses to attack, in this example by spinning in with *uchimata*. Note that uke's head and upper body are tightly controlled by tori's choice of grip.

Fig 54(i) Once the grip is achieved, it is a relatively simple matter to throw uke with *uchimata*. The right leg swings behind and tori pulls him onto his side chest, breaking his balance with *uchimata*. The right leg swings behind and tori pulls him onto his side chest, breaking his balance.

Fig 54(j)   As tori's upper body pulls uke forward and down, tori's left hip blocks his hips as his left leg swings through his.

Fig 54(k)   Tori's left leg sweeps uke into the air as his arms pull him over tori's hip.

Fig 54(l)   As uke falls to the mat, tori pushes down with his arms to ensure that he lands on his back with impetus.

Fig 54(m)   As uke hits the mat, tori can retain his balance or roll over him as needs dictate. In *nage-komi*, or throwing practice, it is sometimes good policy to alternate both styles of finish. *Makikomi* is another alternative, but may be too heavy for most training partners.

GEORGE KERR'S TRAINING FORMULA

In the opinion of my coach, George Kerr, the basis of teaching judo to win tournaments in the intensely competitive modern environment revolves around four basic throws and a sound grounding in *newaza*. This is a controversial concept that will not please the traditionalists in judo. However, it is to the credit of a man so steeped in judo tradition as George is, that he retains a flexible mind and can be so eminently practical.

The four throws are *tai-otoshi*, *osoto-gari*, *ouchi-gari* and *ippon-seoi-nage*. They lend themselves very well to combinations with each other and many other throws. They are the sort of techniques that can always be made to work, whoever the opponent. Their strength lies in the fact that they are the basis of sound judo movement, rather than being mere tricks that rely on the opponent making serious errors of judgement. Particularly useful for smaller men is the *ouchi-gari/tai-otoshi* combination. This was the basis of Kisaburo Watanabe's judo and, when perfected, these two techniques complement one another to devastating effect. Maurice Allen of Scotland, who represented Great Britain in the World Championship in Mexico City in 1969, was a student of George Kerr who used these techniques to good effect, so good in fact that he was able to win a world sombo wrestling championship in Moscow.

Having said that these four throws form the basis of competitive success does not reduce judo or the individual judoka in any way. I practised *seoi-nage* dutifully for many years, but never had any real success with it, being tall and unable to bend my knees with sufficient dexterity to master the technique. We often begin training sessions with numerous repetitions of *uchikomi* and *nage-komi* on *morote-seoi-nage*, and this did have a spin-off benefit in the end, developing hand/feet coordination and good rotating ability.

In contests of minor importance, such as

Fig 55   Marc Alexandre, the French lightweight champion, who won the Olympic title in Seoul, on his way to winning just the bronze medal in Los Angeles. Notice his relaxed but balanced posutre as he comes to grips with Britain's Stephen Gawthorpe. An *uchimata* specialist, experience shows just in the way he stands.

local and area championships, George would handicap me for the first 4 minutes, insisting I only use *seoi-nage* attacks, although in the last minute I could use anything, and often had to, my *seoi-nage* worked so rarely! Luckily though, I was able to do the other three techniques as well as *uchimata*, which had been my *tokui-waza* in my early days, so I had the right base to proceed from. Over the years, as I met more and more difficult opposition, I had to develop other methods too, but these were the core of what made me effective in contest.

The hallmarks of non-Japanese style judo are the belt-gripping tactics so favoured by

Soviet judoka. The unexpected pick-ups and leg grabs as epitomized by Robert van de Walle and the inexorable *juji-gatame* roll, popularized by some great Russian champions, notably Iaskevitch. The same technique was executed to perfection by one of the world's top exponents of brilliant *tachiwaza*, Neil Adams of Great Britain, in the u78k category of the 1981 World Championships final, when he devastated the Japanese, Jiro Kase.

The 1981 World Championships in Maastricht in Holland was doubly remarkable from the point of view of *newaza* because of the presence of Katsuhiko Kashiwazaki of Japan whose turnover of *obi-tori-gaeshi* into *osaekomi-waza* was every bit as unstoppable as Adams' *juji-gatame*. The present contest rules do not really favour *newaza* experts, as the conduct of judo matches is very much geared to spectator appeal and *newaza* is not felt to be particularly interesting. To be decisive in modern judo, *newaza* must immediately exploit any weakness or mistake of the opponent. This has lead to big changes in the way that *newaza* is practised in club dojo, generally of a negative kind; the amount of time devoted to the study of *newaza* has diminished almost directly in proportion to the importance it is given in contest.

Paradoxically, though, as people are increasingly difficult to surprise and catch with trick techniques in *tachiwaza*, the most successful champions have to resort to developing decisive *newaza* with which to defeat awkward opponents. Even the most brilliant players can no longer rely on *tachiwaza* if they wish to endure as champions. Hitoshi Sugai of Japan is a case in point. The World Champion in 1985 and 1987, he was a champion in the best Japanese tradition; sharp gripping, a supple body and fast feet combined to produce a laser-fast *uchimata* that was more than even the world's best fighters could cope with. Time and again, he threw his opponents for ippon, yet, by the 1988 Olympics, his judo had been taped and he was ignominiously grappled out of contention in his first round

contest by the tall Frenchman Stephane Traineau. A year later, in the 1989 World Championships, the French fighter once again proved to be his nemesis, this time more decisively, clambering on his back after a failed *uchimata* attempt and applying a *juji-gatame* which looked as inevitable as it did painful.

THE CONTEST TECHNIQUES OF PETER SEISENBACHER

Attacking Techniques

In the early days of my judo career, my natural feeling was for *uchimata*, the inner-thigh throw, probably because I was strong in the upper body and usually able to bend people over and then use my long legs to throw them. My *uchimata* was always of the hopping, leggy *ken-ken* variety, rather than the precision hip technique favoured by so many top Japanese fighters. Against stronger fighters whom I could not bend, I had to develop other techniques to defeat them. *Ouchi-gari* was a natural paired technique for *uchimata*, and later *tai-otoshi* proved useful as well. I also had a variety of more opportunistic trick techniques including *ko-uchi-gari*, leg grabs and *nidan kosoto-gari*, as well as some standing armlock attacks. However, as far as *tachiwaza* was concerned, *osoto-gari* was the key to my international judo success. From this technique, or from the threat of it, proceeded many of my most memorable ippons.

The techniques in this chapter were honed in *randori* for use in contest. Self-defence, as such, was never a consideration in my training, although a throw that could work on Vitali Pesniak of the Soviet Union or Fabien Canu of France would presumably be effective in any self-defence context. I have chosen to present the techniques, together with some of the unexpected occurrences that accompanied them, more or less as they occurred in the learning experience I underwent. Sometimes things went exactly as planned, at other times nothing went as expected. The unpredictability of judo is one of its most exciting aspects, and one of the things that makes determination coupled to an ability to react and adapt, such important factors in one's judo development.

In *randori*, as in contest, I aimed to build my judo around my *osoto-gari*. After the World Championships in 1983, I had a lot of re-building to do. I had lost first to Canu and then to Nose of Japan, whom the Frenchman had also beaten. I was extremely tired when I fought Nose and he defeated me very decisively throwing me first for waza-ari with *uchimata* and, as I stood up, still retaining the same grip, he threw me again immediately, marking a second waza-ari and taking the bronze medal. Once I was beaten, the World Championships did not matter for me. I forgot the bad result immediately and began working on a new plan against my opponents for the Olympics, not in the least discouraged.

I learned something from every contest. One problem with *osoto-gari* is that it is not a safe technique in the way that drop *seoi* or *tai-otoshi* are. The risk factor is high. It may succeed spectacularly and it may equally well be countered spectacularly. Time and again, I had to adapt the technique to my opponent. One of the most obvious dangers was that of being countered with *osoto-gaeshi*, a very basic move taught to beginners where *osoto* is countered by *osoto*. The Japanese were very good at this, some using a variant that involved stepping back into a *harai-goshi*. The Russians, though, were among the most dangerous fighters to attack with *osoto-gari* or indeed any one-legged throw.

The effectiveness of such techniques generally depends upon close body contact, but giving such contact to a Bodavelli or a Pesniak could be disastrous. Pesniak was an exceptionally dangerous opponent. He gave the impression of being relaxed and indifferent in contest, but could explode into action in a quite unpredictable way and score ippon. I used to call him a sleeping dragon because of

Fig 56   The great danger for all *osoto-gari* specialists!

the danger which he represented that was not obvious to the spectator. We had many interesting battles which reached a level almost like physical chess.

The main change I had to make was to stop gripping over the top with my strong left arm and try more to go for the undergrasp. This was the only valid strategy when faced with opponents who were too upright and strong to pull down into a vulnerable bent-over posture.

(a)

(b)

(c)

Osoto-Gari *Fig 57(a)–(c)*
This sequence demonstrates the danger of being picked up when attacking with a conventional *osoto-gari*.

Fig 57(a)   Tori launches his *osoto-gari* from long range but uke can easily turn into him and block the attack.

Fig 57(b)   Uke drops his right arm around tori's waist, bending his knees and keeping his back straight.

Fig 57(c)   It is a relatively easy matter for uke to throw tori with *uranage* by straightening his legs and lifting tori over his shoulder.

I found that the best method to attack pick-up specialists such as the top Russians was not to aim for chest contact but, rather, to drive the left hand against my opponent's head and push my arms straight, keeping a gap between us. I was still able to throw by driving my opponent over his blocked leg but it was much more difficult for him to try and pick me up. The direction of the attack would generally be determined by his stance and the way in which he attempted to defend. The throw would then become classified as an *osoto-gake*.

Osoto-Gake *Fig 58(a)–(c)*
Fig 58(a)   A conventional *osoto-gake*, aiming to throw uke directly to his rear.
Fig 58(b)   *Osoto-gake*, this time hooking and driving uke obliquely to the rear.
Fig 58(c)   Note how the foot pins uke in place as tori's hands drive uke over his trapped leg.

(a)

(b)

(c)

The best-laid plans of mice and men, and even Olympic champions, sometimes go astray. In the Matsumae Cup, in celebration of the inauguration of the Budo Centre in Vienna in 1984, I was at the peak of my prowess and confidence and the reigning Olympic Champion. I went out to face my old rival, Pesniak, and attacked him with *osoto-gake*, only to be spectacularly dumped for ippon in front of my home crowd.

Countering Osoto-Gari with O-Goshi
Fig 59(a)-(h)
This sequence demonstrates the unusual method Pesniak employed to take me by surprise and score a spectacular victory.

Fig 59(a)   Uke begins to attack with left *osoto-gari*.

Fig 59(b)   Tori, rather than attempt a conventional *osoto-gari* counter attack, takes a big step inwards with his right foot, pivoting on his left foot and slips his right hip underneath uke's descending left hip at the buttock.

Fig 59(c)   Tori slips his right arm around uke's waist and, pulling with his left arm, draws him onto his right hip.

Fig 59(d)   By pulling with both arms, rotating at the waist and straightening the legs, tori lifts uke clear of the ground.

Fig 59(e)   Uke is hoisted onto tori's hip, completely airborne and about to go over for ippon.

Fig 59(f)   A straightforward *o-goshi* action swings uke over tori's hip.

(a)

(b)

(c)

(d)

(e)

(f)

(g)

Fig 59(g)   Uke has nowhere to go but down.
Fig 59(h)   Tori completes the throw by releasing uke with his right arm.

The Pesniak Controversy

This technique is unconventional and very effective. Pesniak's body movement was the opposite of what I had anticipated. Such surprises often succeed spectacularly. Some *seoinage* specialists counter *osoto-gari* with *seoinage* in just the same way, using their hip as a fulcrum to block the attacking leg as it strikes, allowing them to get right under to counter.

Sato once said that when you win a World Championship it is for one day only; if the event were held again the following day, the results would surely be different. This is clearly true. One of the great beauties of judo is that it allows you to plan your strategy to exploit your opponent's weaknesses.

After my shock defeat by Pesniak in the

(h)

Fig 60(a)   This was the controversial sequence that took Seisenbacher past Vitaly Pesniak (Soviet Union), one of his strongest opponents, on his way to the World Title in 1985 in Seoul. He attacked Pesniak with *osoto-gari* and blocked, putting his right leg through to kill the action totally.

Fig 60(b)   Pesniak appeared to reap – an illegal action from that position – and was given a keikoku penalty.

Fig 60(d)   He hit the ground squarely on his back for an incontestable ippon.

Fig 60(c)   Shortly afterwards, Seisenbacher attacked again with *osoto-gari*. Pesniak started to block in the same manner, but then remembered the penalty, and withdrew the leg – putting himself in the perfect position for Seisenbacher's technique.

Matsumae Cup, we next met in the semifinals of the World Championships the following year in Seoul. In the first 30 seconds, I attacked immediately, ready to adapt the direction of my *osoto-gari* into a *harai-goshi* type action if he attempted to turn square to counter me the same way once again. As I did this, he reacted instinctively when his counter was suddenly rendered ineffective and blocked my throwing action with a reflexive, but illegal move.

Osoto-Gari Illegally Blocked *Fig 61(a)–(d)*
Fig 61(a)   Tori attacks with *osoto-gari*, uke blocks by placing the back of his calf against the front of tori's shin.
Fig 61(b)   Tori strives to throw uke and he blocks him forcefully, pushing tori to his front.
Fig 61(c)   Tori loses his balance and falls, but the block and uke's intention to throw him on his front are both illegal actions.
Fig 61(d)   Tori ends up on his front, but the attack earns him the advantage and uke is penalized with a keikoku.

(a)

(b)

(c)

(d)

This put me in a very high-pressure situation. I was in the semifinal of the World Championships against one of my fiercest rivals, leading by a waza-ari with virtually the whole contest to run. There was only one thing to do, go all out to finish it. If I had tried to play safe and hold on to my lead I would surely have come unstuck. I attacked with the same technique again, harder and faster than the first time.

Osoto-Gari into Harai-Goshi *Fig 62(a)–(f)*
Fig 62(a)   Tori attacks with *osoto-gari* again. Uke's instinct is to defend in the same way again.
Fig 62(b)   His defence falters as he realizes that he will be disqualified if he repeats the illegal action. He removes his blocking leg.
Fig 62(c)   His indecision costs him the contest. Tori is too far through with his left leg to be stopped now.

(a)

(b)

(c)

(d)

(e)

(f)

Fig 62(d) Tori's left arm goes around uke's head and he pins him to his body as he reaps away uke's leg and dives for the floor.

Fig 62(e) Uke is completely up-ended and has no hope of recovery.

Fig 62(f) Ippon. He is thrown flat on his back.

It is interesting that many spectators watching that contest thought that I had smashed Pesniak with the second attack because his unfair tactics had angered me in the first instance. This was not the case. I made a calculated decision to bring a potentially very dangerous situation to a speedy conclusion, and the gamble paid off.

I developed *osoto-gari* against people that I could not bend and always used it most effectively against right-handed players who thought that they were safe with their weight on the back leg. I never used it against left-handed fighters, preferring *uchimata* and *ouchi-gari*, which worked particularly well for me. It proved to be the perfect combination for the other basic techniques which were the foundation of my judo: *tai-otoshi*, *uchimata* and *ouchi-gari*. Initially, I did both *tai-otoshi* and *uchimata* from the fairly high collar grip, keeping the left arm bent as a defence against *seoi-nage*. This is vitally important for taller fighters especially to remember. Walking around with the higher grip and waiting to see what develops is particularly dangerous. If you favour the higher grip, attack with it at the first opportunity and be aware at all times of the danger represented by a left *seoi-nage*. My personal philosophy, whenever I fought in a big competition, was to finish the weaker opposition, often those I came up against early in the day, as quickly as possible in order to conserve energy. I would set out to dominate from the word go and either throw or demoralize my opponents and make them wish to give up, or *reignien*, as we say in Austria.

When my opponents stand one-side on and keep one foot back, I generally do *osoto-gari*, but those who brace and stand solid I throw with *tai-otoshi*. In the Los Angeles Olympic final, I threw the American, Berland, for ippon with my *tai-otoshi*. Generally, I did it two ways, neither of which much resembled my ideal, which was the *tai-otoshi* of Neil Adams whom I thought had the best *tai-otoshi* in the world. Mine was not the supple under and over sort of technique, but relied more on blocking my opponent's leg and a powerful upper body rotation to down him. The major variations were in the use of the left arm.

Seisenbacher's First Version of Tai-Otoshi
Fig 63(a)–(g)

This worked well against people whom I could make bend over, or who preferred to defend from this posture:

Fig 63(a) Uke is crouching and trying to keep tori out by defending with stiff arms. Tori has an overgrasp high on uke's collar with his left hand and he is gripping uke's right sleeve at the biceps with his left hand. Tori leans on him to make uke even more tense than he is.

Fig 63(b) Tori relaxes his left shoulder and throws his arm over uke's right shoulder and around his neck as tori jumps straight into *tai-otoshi*. There are no complicated steps, tori just positions himself to uke's right, and then jumps.

Fig 63(c) Tori lands with his feet evenly spaced and his weight equally distributed over both feet. Tori's left arm pulls uke's head into his upper side chest, as the right arm pulls uke's sleeve into tori's waist.

Fig 63(d) Concentrating on keeping his weight going forwards, tori pulls uke's head down and rotates him down and over his outstretched, and virtually straight, left leg.

Fig 63(e) Tori throws uke by punching the left hand to the floor, pivoting at the waist as he makes a big turn of the shoulders.

Fig 63(f) Note that tori's left knee is almost touching the mat at the finish and the degree of hip turn necessary for a good throw.

Fig 63(g) Tori follows up with *kesa-gatame*, in case ippon is not scored.

(a)

(b)

(c)

(d)

(e)

(f)

(g)

Seisenbacher's Second Version of Tai-Otoshi
Fig 64(a)–(g) (This is more orthodox.)

Fig 64(a)   Tori has a conventional left under-grasp and pushes uke to get a reaction from him.

Fig 64(b)   As tori feels uke stiffen and adopt a defensive posture, tori steps in close to uke's right foot with his left foot, pivots on it and rotates his right hip anti-clockwise so that his right foot comes down next to uke's right foot.

Fig 64(c)   Tori bends his knees and pulls down with his right hand, drawing uke against his side chest with his left hand as he begins his stab across with the left foot.

Fig 64(d)   Tori reaches as far as possible with the left foot and snatches uke's body into contact with his own.

Fig 64(e)   Tori bends at the waist and punches the left hand towards the mat, pulling uke over his outstretched left leg.

Fig 64(f)   Tori finishes the technique by straightening his left arm, in effect punching uke into the mat.

Fig 64(g)   Uke is thrown for ippon.

(a)

(b)

(c)

(d)

(e)

(f)

(g)

Uchimata was for a long time my *tokuiwaza* and worked very well against the crouching, stiff, defensive type of fighter I came up against at national and European level. Japanese competitors were much more difficult to throw with this technique because of their generally greater leg and hip flexibility. Al-though later I used the throw from the same grip as my *osoto-gari* (left hand at the collar bone, right hand holding the sleeve at the biceps), originally I held with the right hand on the outside of my opponent's left sleeve at the elbow. The left hand gripped deep at the back of the neck, giving good head control.

Uchimata *Fig 66(a)–(f)*

Fig 66(a)   Tori throws himself into the attack, stepping in deep between uke's legs on his left foot and then pivoting and throwing in his right foot.

Fig 66(b)   Tori transfers all his weight onto his right leg and drives the left upwards, so that the inside of his upper thigh lifts uke's leg. Tori's right arm pulls his arm into his waist as the elect pulls him forwards and off-balance.

Fig 65   Bernard Tchoullyan again, this time throwing Neilsen of Norway with right *uchimata* in the 1981 World Championships. These two throws, *uchimata* and *seoi-nage*, when combined on opposite sides, make a devastating double threat.

(a)

(b)

Fig 66(c) Tori twists his upper body around through 90 degrees, turning to his right, pulling all the time and hopping in order to jack uke up so that he is forced off-balance over his own supporting leg.

Fig 66(d) As tori pulls and continues to rotate, he dips his head towards the floor and his position becomes completely unstable.

Fig 66(e) As uke falls over the outside edge of his foot, tori turns his shoulders and springs into the technique.

Fig 66(f) The fall is a heavy one and tori lands completely on top of uke.

Sometimes in contest the sheer energy and commitment put into the technique meant I landed with my left hip on my opponent's head, which was not a very nice experience for him, but taught him to respect the technique.

Ouchi-Gari

Fear of being thrown with *uchimata* often made my opponents adopt radical stances and the threat of the technique was useful for provoking them to make big reactions which I could exploit with other techniques. One of the moves which worked best for me because it combined so well with *osoto-gari* and *tai-otoshi* also was *o-uchi-gari*. It is very interesting that these four techniques, which formed the basis of my judo, were also the same techniques that Yasuhiro Yamashita utilized most often in his judo. Like me, Yamashita was a left-handed fighter and, also like me, he could not do *seoi-nage*, which just goes to show that even the best judo men still have something to learn!

Behind every attack is the danger of a counter as Figs 67 and 68 show.

Fig 67   In the Commonwealth Games event, 1986, in Edinburgh, Andrew Richardson of Australia (502) has attacked Kevin Docherty (Canada) without breaking balance and finds himself on the end of a strong *kosoto-gari* type counter, using the thigh. He fell heavily.

Fig 68   In the European Championships in Rostock, East Germany, in 1982, Janos Gyani met the great French middleweight Bernard Tchoullyan. He attacked with a footsweep, but was countered with a superb *tsubame-gaeshi* by the French champion.

121

O-Uchi-Gari *Fig 69(a)–(g)*

Fig 69(a) Tori takes his orthodox left-hand undergrip and lets uke feel that he is going to attack with *tai-otoshi* or *uchimata*.

Fig 69(b) Tori throws his left leg across in front of uke and simultaneously steps behind with the left and makes a strong pull to the front. The aim of this action is to get uke to resist strongly to the threat of a forward throw and brace himself by putting his weight on his left foot. Depending on how nervous a fighter he is, it may or may not be necessary to turn the head to get him to react as required.

Fig 69(c) As tori feels that uke's weight distribution is as he wants it, tori reverses the direction of his spin, using his initial half-turn almost as a springboard to push off against and bounce back. Tori's right leg supports his balance at this point, but his body-weight is hanging on uke.

Fig 69(d) Pulling himself into uke strongly, tori inserts his foot between uke's legs and clips him as low on the calf as possible with his own lower leg. Tori continues to turn into uke and drives his weight backwards by pushing with his right leg as he opens his hips.

Fig 69(e) This is a close-up of the contact for *o-uchi-gari*, from the opposite view. Note the contact is almost ankle to ankle.

Fig 69(f) As uke loses balance, tori lunges into the throw with total commitment and drive towards the floor.

Fig 69(g) As they go down, tori retains control by steering uke onto his back with his hands. Note how uke's right shoulder is controlled by the left-hand lapel grip and his left arm by tori's right hand.

(a)

(b)

(c)

(d)

(e and f)

(g)

123

When a judo player becomes well known as a thrower, the opposition do whatever they can to frustrate his attempts to grip and attack. Often this takes the form of refusing to grip up and much time is spent preventing the possibility of a two-handed grip being taken. The rules are constantly being changed to frustrate negative defensive action of this kind, and the increase in the size of the jackets helps with the initial gripping. But it is important to have appropriate 'smaller' techniques for dealing with these types of situation more easily. Such techniques tend to be useful tactically, also, as they allow you to make point-scoring attacks without taking the kind of total risk of exposing yourself to a counter, as happens when you try *osoto-gari* or *uchimata*. My aim was always to try and win by ippon, whatever the contest, but against particularly awkward opposition it was often necessary to be unorthodox. With my relatively long arms and legs I liked *ko-uchi-gari* in conjunction with the leg grab, a technique sometimes known as *kuchiki tao-oshi* or dead tree fall.

Kuchiki Tao-Oshi *Fig 70(a)–(d)*

Fig 70(a)   From a one-handed grip, standing side on to uke, tori gathers the cloth at the lapel and steps between uke's legs with his left leg, aiming to clip uke just behind the heel with his left foot.

Fig 70(b)   The normal reaction is for uke to move his left foot as he feels the threat of *ko-uchi-gari*. By pushing the cloth of his jacket into his face as tori lunges into him, I can guarantee a reaction. As I see his foot move, I reach to grab his leg.

Fig 70(c)   Tori catches uke's leg with his left hand and pulls it towards him as he pushes uke down with his left hand.

Fig 70(d)   If tori has the element of surprise, the technique may score quite well but, more often than not, uke is able to spin out to some extent. However, even the koka and the yuko, although they should never be the ultimate aim of the judoka, ought not be despised. They can be useful advantages in a contest and may lead to more fruitful possibilities.

(a)

(b)

(c)

(d)

Unorthodox techniques can be spectacularly successful when all else fails. Standing armlocks fall into this category and there have been some moments of real judo drama as a result of them. Probably the most memorable incident was in the 1985 World Championships heavyweight final, when the South Korean, Chong-yul Cho, delighted the home crowd by defeating Hitoshi Saito of Japan with a viciously effective *waki-gatame*. Curiously, standing armlocks are very rare in Japanese dojos. There seems to be a tacit agreement between Japanese judoka not to use them, although occasionally a fighter does emerge who seems to have a penchant for them such as Nobutoshi Hikage, the 1983 and 1985 World Champion. Japanese unfamiliarity with these techniques makes them slightly more susceptible than they might otherwise be, but it is a mistake to assume that they are easily caught by them. Saito was much too over-confident when he went out to meet Cho and the result was one that might have occurred only perhaps once in a hundred meetings. The fact that it was the final of the World Championships was just unfortunate for Saito.

The great controversy with standing armlocks always stems from the rule that disallows the attacker from applying an armlock and then throwing his opponent. However, current interpretation seems to allow this technique, which was much used by one of my early heroes and rivals, Detlef Ultsch of East Germany. The trick with the technique is to keep the arm straight as you attack the opponent with *uchimata*, and only begin to apply the kind of pressure needed to earn a submission when he is sprawling forwards on the ground. Making the transition rapidly and smoothly without injuring the opponent takes a lot of control and skill. Such techniques are inevitably controversial, but there is no denying their effectiveness.

A Standing Armlock *Fig 71(a)–(g)*

Fig 71(a)   Uke is holding one-handed and is reluctant to allow tori to grip him with his right hand and he keeps his left sleeve well back from tori. Tori has his left hand under uke's stiff, defensive right arm. Tori takes hold of uke's right hand with his right hand and turns his left hand upwards, twisting his forearm to straighten uke's arm.

Fig 71(b)   Tori turns away from uke and pulls him forward, extending uke's arm.

Fig 71(c)   Tori quickly throws his right leg back, placing his foot between uke's feet.

Fig 71(d)   Tori attacks with left *uchimata*.

(a)

(b)

(c)

(d)

A Follow-On Opportunity

Fig 71(e) Tori springs into uke strongly, lifting him off the ground with the action of his left hip and causing him to sprawl forwards.

Fig 71(f) Uke is very unsteady and has to put out his left arm to save himself. Note that his right arm is completely extended.

Fig 71(g) Now, with uke on the ground, tori attempts to get the submission and apply the pressure as quickly as possible against his elbow joint. It is also possible at this juncture to step over his head with the left leg and sit down into *juji-gatame*, but *waki-gatame* is perhaps quicker.

Note Tori must show an intention of throwing his opponent, otherwise he may be penalized.

Fig 71(h) The leverage position the grip affords on the elbow is good, but it is possible at this stage to switch to a controversial *waki-gatame* grip if desired.

(e)

(f)

(g)

(h)

127

Renrakuwaza: Combination Techniques

Once the judoka has mastered the basic attacking techniques with which he feels comfortable, the task becomes one of learning to make linked attacks and to develop combination techniques, so that even the most determined defence can be opened up and dismantled. *Osoto* was the key to many of the combinations which were most effective for me. By linking it with the other throws that I could do in practice, it was usually possible to find a weak point in even the strongest judoka's defences. The missing throw in my repertoire, from the ideal point of view, was *seoi-nage*, but even so I could normally find a way to make the others work by using them in combination and changing the order with which I applied the techniques. Combination techniques tend to be classified as *renrakuwaza* or *renzokuwaza*. The difference lies in whether the second technique carries on in the direction of the first or whether there is a complete switch. *Ouchi-gari* into *tai-otoshi*, for example, would be *renrakuwaza*; right *uchimata* followed by left *seoi-nage*, on the other hand, would be *renzokuwaza*.

Osoto-gari into Tai-otoshi *Fig 72(a)–(f)*

Fig 72(a) A *kenka-yotsu* (opposing grips) situation. Tori has a left hold, but grips the end of his opponent's sleeve rather than the cloth at the biceps as he feels he has a better chance with *tai-otoshi*. Uke is holding right and tori bears down upon him to get him to react by pulling up.

Fig 72(b) Tori makes a strong attack with *osoto-gari* against uke's rear leg.

(a)

(d)

128

Fig 72(c) Uke reacts by throwing his left leg back, out of range of tori's attacking leg, and stiffening his left arm.

Fig 72(d) Rather than oppose uke's stiff left arm, tori simply pulls it around his waist as he swings his right leg behind him. As tori's shoulders begin to turn, tori's arm just wraps around tori's waist.

Fig 72(e) Tori transfers his weight onto his right foot and, bending his knee, stabs across in front of uke with his left leg, aiming to contact with the back of his ankle against the front of uke's shin near the ankle. As tori's upper body rotates, he pulls down with the right hand and round with the left.

Fig 72(f) As uke goes over tori's outstretched leg, tori punches his left hand into the ground, ensuring an aggressive, decisive finish to the technique.

(b)

(c)

(e)

(f)

The most important thing with attacking judo is the ability to switch depending upon how your opponent reacts. Although *tai-otoshi* may sometimes be the perfect combination with which to follow up an *osoto-gari*, at other times it will be better to do something else. There are numerous possibilities, but basically everything depends on your opponent's reaction. Some people, when pressed, push back, others move, others attempt to attack without waiting to see what develops; you must have an answer for all of these situations. When faced with an opponent who attempts to skip out of range rather than block, the following technique can work effectively. It is also very useful against judoka who lurk in wait for the *osoto-gari* in the hope of doing the traditional *osoto-gaeshi*.

(a)

Osoto-Gari into Kosoto-Gari *Fig 73(a)–(g)*
Fig 73(a)   In a *kenka-yotsu* (opposing grips) situation, uke is aware of the danger from tori's *osoto-gari* and is trying to keep well out of his reach. Tori attacks with *osoto-gari*. Uke already has his left leg well back so he cannot withdraw it, and tori pins his weight on that leg.
Fig 73(b)   The attack is a real one, both hands are working, the left in particular pushing uke's head back.
Fig 73(c)   As tori attacks, uke cannot move his left leg so he has to react by stepping back with his right leg. As tori feels him beginning to step, he puts his left foot on the floor and transfers his weight to his left leg.
Fig 73(d)   As uke steps, tori steps, bringing his right leg through to do *kosoto-gari*.
Fig 73(e)   Tori continues to push with his left hand as his right leg goes around behind uke.
Fig 73(f)   Tori sweeps away uke's feet with *kosoto-gari* before he can recover his balance.
Fig 73(g)   Tori controls the finish of the technique by using his hands to steer uke to the mat and ensure that he goes flat on his back. The momentum of the attack normally means a lot of ground is covered and the score is normally a high one.

(d)

(b)

(c)

(e)

(f)

(g)

Kaeshiwaza: Counter Techniques

As a competitor, I was always an attacking player who looked for the opportunity to throw my opponents for ippon. As such, I did not make a special study of *kaeshiwaza* or counter techniques as many fighters do, preferring to take the initiative rather than wait for my opponent to bring the fight to me. However, *kaeshiwaza* are an important area for study. One technique I did develop as a consequence of practising so much in Japan, where many players use *seoi-nage*, was a *tani-otoshi* type take-down. This is a very easy technique to develop and does not require a high level of skill to be effective. However, good *newaza* is advantageous as it allows tori to fully exploit any advantage.

A Tani-Otoshi Type Take-down *Fig 74(a)– (d)*

Fig 74(a)   Uke begins his attack with *ippon-seoi-nage*. As uke turns in, tori places his hand on the side of uke's back, slowing the speed of his turn.

Fig 74(b)   Having stopped uke's turn, tori leans diagonally to his left front and pushes uke in that direction, breaking his balance before he can begin to turn out.

Fig 74(c)   As tori pushes, I drop my body-weight rapidly, preventing him from getting underneath me with his attack.

Fig 74(d)   I drop to my knee and pull him to the floor where I have the advantage in *newaza*.

(a)

(c)

(b)

(d)

Newaza

In the modern world, where people more and more seem to have less and less time, *newaza* does not receive the attention it deserves. Even champions tend to specialize. There are a vast number of techniques used in *newaza*, but each of us has to discover the ones that work best, given our individual strengths and weaknesses. The serious competitor has to concentrate on developing match-winning techniques and enough awareness to at least avoid making silly mistakes, if not eradicating all weak points. It is no coincidence that many great champions have won their titles through *newaza* superiority.

Newaza is something that takes time and a lot of practice. Natural talent or flair counts for a lot more in *tachiwaza*. In *newaza*, it is easier for the less gifted to make progress and, if you are physically strong, to use that to your advantage. Confidence in *newaza* is vital, if you are to have effective standing techniques and practice really can make perfect. Neil Adams was a master in *newaza*, as was his inspiration for *juji-gatame*, the Russian, Iaskevitch. The Japanese have also produced their experts, men like Sato, Kashiwazaki and Yamashita, whose ability is so highly developed that they make the remarkable seem commonplace. As in *tachiwaza*, the key to success is repetition and combinations. You have to know how your opponent will try to defend before you make an attack so that you can exploit his reaction.

My *newaza* was transformed by the amount of time I spent practising in Japanese dojos. The western style is typified by the *juji-gatame* attack against an opponent defending on all fours. In Japanese dojos, practice tends to be conducted with one partner taking up a seated position and inviting his opponent to come between his legs and attack. Each time a point is scored, the two alternate. As a result of this style of practice, the Japanese tend to be very adept at applying techniques if they get you between their legs. Equally they are alert to the dangers when they find themselves in that situation. When attacking a prone opponent, they tend to favour *shimewaza* and turnovers into *newaza*. Generally speaking, the level of *newaza* is much higher in Japan than in the West. If they have a particular weakness, it tends to be that they do not defend against *juji-gatame* so well, as they are attacked less with it. Their *shimewaza* are lethal and it is not prudent to take up a face-down position in order to defend against a Japanese opponent unless you know his *newaza* is weak. My personal speciality in *newaza* were always *juji-gatame*, but I experimented with certain other techniques, such as Kashiwazaki's *obi-tori-gaeshi*. I also developed some techniques in Japan, which were necessary for survival in Japanese dojos.

One of the secrets of good *newaza* is to give people lots of opportunities to make mistakes. You have to use your intelligence to outsmart your opponents much more so than in standing work. The problem with the way a lot of people practise *newaza* is that they divorce it from contest reality. The chance to go into *newaza* happens in contest from a take-down situation or from a half-successful throw, or when a throw is blocked and both fighters go to the ground. People rarely practise in this way. *Newaza* sessions tend to be separate and the class often spends all the time on the ground. Little or no effort is made to avoid techniques by standing up and so when it happens in contest, as it inevitably does, it is a new situation and the judoka who wants to do *newaza*, who has the advantage, may find he loses it because he does not know how to keep his opponent down. These points should be borne in mind when developing techniques or coaching *newaza* to classes.

Drop *seoi-nage* is a problematic technique to deal with because the attacker is able to come in so low and fast and on-balance and, if he is unsuccessful, can quickly curl up and defend or try to stand up or crawl out of the competition area, but this is one possible solution to the problem.

(a)

Drop Seoi-Nage Countered by Juji-Gatame
Fig 75(a)–(m)

Fig 75(a)   Uke attacks with *seoi-nage*, and tori defends by placing his hand on uke's lower back, dropping his weight and smothering the attack.

Fig 75(b)   Tori sits on uke's lower back, squashing his attack, and uke senses the danger of being trapped in a disadvantageous *newaza* position.

Fig 75(c)   As uke tries to crawl away, tori jumps on his back as if he were mounting a horse.

Fig 75(d)   Tori hooks his left foot inside uke's left thigh and reaches under uke's right arm with his right arm.

Fig 75(e)   Tori takes his weight on his left hand and rolls onto his right side, turning uke with him by levering up with his left leg, so that uke's hips have to turn.

(b)

(c)

(d)

(e)

135

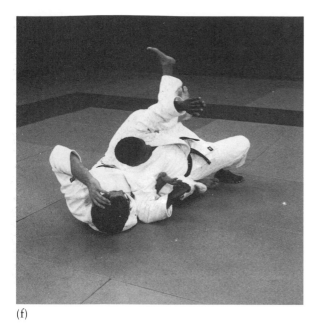

(f)

(g)

(h)

(i)

Fig 75(f)   Tori rolls onto his side and, as uke turns over, tori is alert to any openings for strangles, etc.

Fig 75(g)   Initially, tori controls uke's right arm with his right arm and uke's lower body with his legs.

Fig 75(h)   Uke clasps his hand to defend against the threat of the armlock, but tori places the side of his forearm against his neck.

Fig 75(i)   Tori swings his left leg up over uke's head and uses his forearm to push uke's head under it.

(j)

(k)

(l)

(m)

Fig 75(j)   With uke's head controlled by the back of tori's thigh, tori can now flatten him out and work on straightening the arm.

Fig 75(k)   Keeping his right arm in position, tori then reaches through with his left hand and grabs his own right lapel.

Fig 75(l)   Tori levers back against uke's arm and leans back, adding his body-weight, the pressure being exerted by muscular exertion.

Fig 75(m)   The arm straightens and uke is forced to submit.

137

Another Version of Juji-Gatame *Fig 76(a)–(l)*
This version of *juji-gatame* is designed for those opponents who try to curl into a ball and stay tight.

Fig 76(a) Tori hooks his feet inside uke's legs and slips his right hand under uke's armpit to grab his right wrist.
Fig 76(b) Tori takes his weight on his left hand, so that he can move smoothly but keep uke under control.
Fig 76(c) Tori places his forehand on the mat . . .
Fig 76(d) . . . and drives his knee into the side of uke's head.
Fig 76(e) Tori places his left fist on his right knee, forming a bar with tori's forearm that uke cannot bend, however strong he is.
Fig 76(f) Tori turns onto his left side and applies pressure against his arm.
Fig 76(g) Uke may attempt to roll at this point but his head is blocked by tori's knee and tori has a free right hand if he wishes to use it.
Fig 76(h) By continuing to twist and lean back, tori breaks uke's grip and the arm comes free.

(a)

(b)

138

(c)

(d)

(e)

(f)

(g)

(h)

Fig 76(i)   Tori catches uke's wrist with his right hand and pulls the arm straight, applying pressure against the elbow joint.

Fig 76(j)   It is possible that uke may try and escape at this point by doing a forward roll.

Fig 76(k)   Uke rolls . . .

Fig 76(l)   . . . but only into the armlock, as tori controls him adequately with his legs, and he has no choice but to tap or risk injury.

Kashiwazaki's Technique: Yoko-Obi-Tori-Gaeshi *Fig 77(a)–(f) (opposite)*
This technique was developed and perfected by Katsuhiko Kashiwazaki of Japan and I was so impressed by his success with it that I decided to try to build it into my own judo. Its potential is obvious.

Fig 77(a)   From the seated position, facing uke, tori throws his left arm over his left shoulder and grips the belt, thumb inside.
Fig 77(b)   Tori reaches under uke's left arm with his right hand and grabs his arm at the triceps. Tori's left leg is inside his legs, the right is outside.

Fig 77(c)   Tori twists to his left and, as he turns uke's upper body with his shoulders, he flicks uke's leg, using a *sumi-gaeshi* action, with his left leg. Note the right leg bent at 45 degrees and acting as a brace to help tori turn uke over.
Fig 77(d)   As uke rolls onto his back, tori disentangles his left leg by supporting his weight on his right leg.
Fig 77(e)   Tori frees his leg and, turning his hips, gets on top of uke in a position to apply *yoko-shiho-gatame*.
Fig 77(f)   Tori applies *yoko-shiho-gatame* by grasping uke's trousers at the crotch, effectively controlling his hips.

(a)

(b)

(c)

(d)

(e)

(f)

In winning his world title in 1981 and the Kano Cup in 1982, Kashiwazaki had appeared to be unstoppable with this technique, yet no one else appeared to use it. I had some success with it, but never perfected it as a competitor, probably because I did not give it enough time – only about six months practice. It is surprising how long most techniques take to settle down so that they can be used at the highest level of competition. Very often, even after a year or more of regular practice, a new technique can still not be ready for the highest level of competition. It can feel strong in *randori*, and even minor competitions, but minute faults are shown up when facing a good-calibre opponent.

This is exactly what happened to me with this *obi-tori-gaeshi*. I made a basic mistake against Michael Borowski (East Germany) and was trapped in a hold down. The mistake is not to attempt the roll if you are lying flat on your back; it is vital to sit up – otherwise, your opponent can get past the legs relatively easily.

Kata-Gatame Followed by Tate-Shiho-Gatame *Fig 78(a)–(c)*

Fig 78(a) Tori's first mistake, going flat on his back, allowed uke to reduce tori's leverage and get into a good counter-attacking position. The second was not controlling uke's left arm correctly, allowing him to slip it around tori's neck and get head control.

Fig 78(b) Uke applies *kata-gatame* and disentangles his leg.

Fig 78(c) It is then a simple matter for uke to apply *tate-shiho-gatame*.

(a)

(b)

(c)

(a)

(b)

A situation much favoured in Japan is fighting off the back and, because they practise it a lot, they get very good as well at coming around the legs. Therefore, it is necessary to have techniques for coping with this too.

Fighting off the Back *Fig 79(a)–(g)*
Fig 79(a)   Tori is on his back and uke is between his legs.
Fig 79(b)   Uke attempts to come around tori's defence and tries to get his arm around tori's neck as a preliminary to disentangling himself and applying *yoko-shiho-gatame*. Tori catches his arm at the elbow.
Fig 79(c)   Uke comes around tori's legs and starts to settle into his *yoko-shiho-gatame*.
Fig 79(d)   Tori controls uke's left shoulder

with both hands and throws his legs up in the air, crossing them and gripping uke's right arm at the biceps.
Fig 79(e)   Tori pulls down with his legs and pushes with his hand on the side of uke's neck, so that his head is low down near tori's hips and his left arm is pinned straight.
Fig 79(f)   Tori quickly throws his left leg over his neck and grips uke's elbow joint with his right hand.
Fig 79(g) Tori applies *ude-hishigi-ude-gatame* by sitting up and levering down against uke's elbow. It is very important to sit up as this lifts the wrist which is pinned on tori's shoulder and increases the pressure applied to uke's elbow.

(c)

(d)

(e)

(f)

(g)

Yoko-Shiho-Gatame *Fig 80(a)–(i)*
This technique requires speed, timing and confidence.

Fig 80(a)   Uke is between tori's legs and tori grabs his left sleeve with his right hand.
Fig 80(b)   Before uke pulls it free, tori grips his sleeves with both hands.
Fig 80(c)   Tori pulls uke's arm down but, at the same time, drops his left leg defence to entice uke to come round into *yoko-shiho-gatame*.
Fig 80(d)   Uke takes the bait and starts to move into the hold-down.
Fig 80(e)   All the while, Tori has retained his grip on the end of uke's left sleeve and grabs his belt with his free left hand as uke comes around.
Fig 80(f)   Tori thrusts his arm through uke's legs as uke comes around, and pulls uke over his chest as tori begins driving with his legs and rotating to his left.
Fig 80(g)   Tori sustains the initial momentum of uke's scramble to come past his legs.
Fig 80(h)   Tori rolls uke off his chest and onto his back. Without his left hand to brace with, uke cannot prevent tori from rolling him over.
Fig 80(i)   Tori pins uke with *yoko-shiho-gatame*.

(a)

(b)

(c)

(d)

(e)

(f)

(g)

(h)

(i)

TECHNIQUES LOST AND FOUND

Techniques are in and out of fashion all the time in judo, with the major throws, *seoi-nage, uchimata, osoto-gari* and *tai-otoshi* – remaining generally at the forefront. However, very occasionally, someone comes along with a unique way of doing things and something brand new appears. Techniques also fall into disuse and even sometimes disappear. One of the most original and unusual combination techniques I have seen – and I only saw one fighter ever do it, and that was Mikhail Cioc of Romania – was *makikomi* into *waki-gatame*. It arose from a very special sort of situation, but he did the same technique three times in the one event, which was the 1987 European Championships in Paris, and actually scored ippon with it in the first 30 seconds of the final agaisnt Clemens Jehle

of Switzerland, so it was obviously no fluke but something he had trained and planned to perfection. Frequently, big heavyweights roll one another over with *makikomi* for a lesser score such as yuko or waza-ari, and sometimes the person being thrown will avoid being held down by continuing the momentum of the throw and rolling the thrower over his chest. Cioc was relatively small and agile for a heavyweight and had obviously had problems with this situation and so had studied it and developed a plan. Each time he threw an opponent with *makikomi* and they tried to roll him over, he would twist in as he went over and turn against the arm and sit into *waki-gatame* in a supremely simple but skilful way. He had obviously worked hard to perfect this technique and it worked brilliantly for him, winning him his only European gold medal ever. I never saw him or anyone else use it again.

5 Modern Training Methods
By George Kerr

A conventional judo training session, properly conducted and held perhaps three times a week, should provide all the strength and fitness work that anyone training below the level of a national squad member needs. Obviously the principal requirement is that trainees push themselves. The following standard format can be varied according to the judgement of the instructor, but represents a basic teaching plan for the class:

10 minutes stretching and warming up.
10 minutes instruction on a particular technique.
15 minutes *uchi-komi* and *nage-komi*.
40 minutes *randori*.
30 minutes *newaza*.
 5 minutes warming down and stretching.

The above amounts to two hours training time, which is about half an hour longer than the average club practice. In fact, an hour for beginners and one and a half hours for intermediate players is probably about right. This is another difference with Japan as, there, three-hour training sessions are considered quite normal. Some university dojos train twice a day and routinely spend up to five hours a day on the mat, whether in the stifling heat of summer or the chill of the Japanese winter, when special training is felt to be especially productive. These special seasonal training sessions are called *shochugeiko* and *kangeiko*.

With a class of beginners, the above format would have to be altered, simply because fitness levels would be unlikley to be sufficient, and considerably more time would have to be spent teaching basic skills in a formal way. Probably the *randori* and ground-work training time would have to be cut and more instruction given in both areas of the sport. Occasionally, informal talks or presentations might be given on any aspects where individual club members hold expertise. The Budokwai, in the days when it was taught by Mr Leggett, enjoyed talks on Japan by members who had lived there, and also language sessions. The possibilities these days are even more interesting and varied; video tapes might be shown and discussed, slides viewed, and so on. By using knowledgeable people to educate trainees from the beginning of their careers, the right start in judo is ensured.

RANDORI

Randori, which is the core of any judo training session, can be divided into various lengths, a 40-minute block might be broken up into 8 x 5 minute practices, 7 x 6, 10 x 4, or 13 x 3, or any combination of varying lengths, with the intention of getting players to train at variable pace. If you are used to training for 6-minute practices, it takes some time to adjust to suddenly only having half that time in which to weigh up an opponent and deal with him. Normally, it is helpful for the students if the instructor indicates how the *randori* is to be broken up at the beginning.

In a crowded dojo, to avoid the risk of collisions and injuries, the instructor can split the class into two, either by experience or weight, and have half on the mat doing *randori* while the other half do *uchi-komi* around the edges of the mat. This can be particularly helpful prior to a big competition, where it can help trainees to get used to the gaps which occur between contests. If at all possible, it should not become the norm for training sessions to have half the class standing around while the other half works; it is better to train continuously.

As well as planning each individual session, the coach has a responsibility to have a long-term strategy for skill development, but he must strike a balance between imposing the skills he wants his students to learn and allowing them to practise the techniques they naturally prefer to do and feel to be important. In trying to extend the skill range of a particular class, the coach has to be very much a salesman and persuade his students as to the value of studying particular techniques. It is important to be flexible and able to respond to the differing needs of the class, as and when they arise. Judo teaching inevitably involves mixed ability of the most difficult kind – much more so in the West than in Japan, since clubs are often attended by judoka of very different levels – but it can be as satisfying as it is often frustrating when the right formula is applied.

NAGE-KOMI

Nage-komi, or repetition throwing, is an extremely arduous form of fitness training for both the thrower and the person or persons being thrown. Yet it has the advantage of being an excellent way to develop skill. Of course, the tiring effect of *nage-komi* varies according to each throw. *De-ashi-barai*, which is essentially a timing-based throw, will require a lot less energy expenditure than *tai-otoshi* or *ippon-seoi-nage*. The exercise becomes more or less difficult depending on how much effort the thrower puts into each individual technique. There is an analogy with hitting a punch bag, if you pace yourself and place your punches you will use a lot less energy than if you go berserk, hitting it as hard and fast as you possibly can.

However, throwing skills need to be fast and sharp and are best practised early in any training session while you are still fresh, or at the end of training when, although weary, you will be thoroughly warmed up and relaxed as well as able to focus on particular problems you may have experienced with certain individuals or physical types. In an ideal world, throwing skills should be practised in a separate session. In any event, they are best practised in conjunction with *uchi-komi* as it helps to make the latter more meaningful and realistic.

Concentration on what you are doing is very important. There is absolutely no point in switching off mentally and going through the motions as if you were doing a jog. Every repetition you make should be vital and alive and you should be getting feedback from your training partners. Make a point of asking them how techniques feel. Anyone can teach technique, but how do you teach feeling? Sometimes, if you concentrate only on how *you* feel doing a certain technique, you can be misled. It is not so important, particularly in *uchi-komi*, that a technique or throwing position feel powerful to you; your partner has to feel it could be effective. If you make a turn in or attack and he feel completely stable and on balance, there is something lacking in your technique. If you are in position for *tai-otoshi* and thinking, 'this is a strong position', and he is thinking exactly the same about his defence, your throw is unlikely to be effective when you try it in *randori* or contest. This need to feel strong all the time is a problem in western judo and perhaps an over-dependence on weight-training might in part explain it. Feedback may well provide the clue you are needing in order to make a throw really effective.

Another important consideration is that,

when you come to fight in contest, you will have a lot more space than you normally have in *randori*. In the relatively controlled *nage-komi* situation, it is important to try and cover ground and use as much space as possible as this allows maximum force to be transmitted into the throwing action. Too often outside Japan, where dojos tend to be a lot larger and there is ample space, people try to almost throw 'on the spot' as it were and, while there are obviously some advantages to this, it is also important to make use of space when it is available.

In *nage-komi* and *randori*, aim to create a state of confusion so that you can perform a throw with the kind of suddenness that makes it so effective in contest. Throwing skills are not robotic and should not be practised sloppily. Try to make every throw like a knock-out punch; if you do it properly your partner should feel like he is hit by a bolt from the blue.

NEWAZA

Take-downs into *newaza* should be practised regularly also, and make a good way to start off a *newaza* training session. *Newaza* ought to be practised in a similar way to *tachiwaza* in order to develop skill. Turn-overs into hold downs, strangles and armlocks should be developed and practised over and over, until they become fully understood. Holding and escaping should also be practised with partners cooperating trying 50, 60, 70, 80, 90 and 100 per cent to escape and also trying to keep the hold on.

STRENGTH AND CONDITIONING TRAINING

With the inclusion of judo in the Olympics, modern techniques of strength and conditioning training, using running and weight-training, have made it vital that anyone competing at international level in judo be super-

fit and extremely strong. Great strength is vital to top-class judo fighters. It is no secret that almost all the top fighters strength-train using weights. The nature of the judo techniques and the training that was undertaken in the old Kodokan made physical power a less crucial factor than in modern competitive judo. There are those who argue that, to a large extent, techniques worked because of the oppositions' ignorance and inexperience: knowledge was power. Today ju-jitsu-based technqiues relying on surprise and attacking weak points are very appealing to those less well-developed physically, but the modern philosophy is not simply to try and exploit the opponent's weak points, but to be as strong as possible while doing so.

Women and older people, especially, feel more confident in learning self-defence techniques based on speed and co-ordinated movements that do not require the user to develop enormous physical strength. However, top women judoka are first-class athletes in their own right now and many are surprisingly strong. It may not be necessary to be that strong if you need only to be able to throw an untrained attacker, but an experienced, knowledgeable opponent is quite another matter.

Unlike those who attend self-defence classes to acquire a pot-pourri of surprises and tricks to neutralize threatening individuals, the competitive judoka faces adversaries who, like himself have trained to eradicate their weak points. To make his task still more difficult, his opponents will have analysed his techniques on video and will devise strategies to frustrate his intentions. If the opposition are doing all of this as well as training with weights, running and doing circuit training to enhance their performance, no competitor at or above a national squad level can afford to do any less. However, below this level, it is best to concentrate on doing judo for fitness. Judo skill development can actually be when those with relatively little experience turn to the weights as a shortcut to their goal, but many do just that. This statement may surprise some people but the fact is that, done properly, judo training is extremely strenuous and the training effect quite severe. The problem is that most clubs do not train effectively. Training sessions have to be adapted to the level of the individuals taking part. The work should be good quality with importance placed on skill acquisition through *uchi-komi*, *nage-komi* and *randori*, where the emphasis is on speed, style and care. Such *randori* is loose and free and the participants can move in a relaxed way, without losing sight of the fact that they are training for a combat sport. Stiff, hard *randori* tends to lead to defensive tight judo and an increase in injuries.

The maxim, 'maximum effect from minimum effort', is well known in judo, and the arguments about power against techniques are as old as the martial arts themselves. However, it is naive not to recognize that the combination of power with fitness and technique is devastating. Ito Mataemon, the founder of the Tenjin Shin'yo Ryu, in which Jigoro Kano studied, was a famous expert in *atemi-waza* and clearly recognized the need for realism in ju-jitsu. He had this to say on the subject:

'The use of power in ju-jitsu is greatly necessary. But it is only when such power is not used in excess that it stands the test of the principle of ju. Another aspect of the use of power must be borne in mind too. From the early stages of a trainee's development in ju-jitsu he must always be careful to avoid reliance on physical strength, for such is an obstacle in the way of his progress towards the gaining of skill in technique. After the trainee has developed a creditable technique, however, then the use of power is acceptable, and in fact absolutely necessary to his effectivness in dealing with an adversary.'

This is very much the modern view with regard to contest effectiveness. Simply being physically stronger than an opponent is not a guarantee of victory but being unnecessarily weaker is an invitation to defeat. The balance in training needs to be correct.

Weight-Training

Weight-training is an extremely popular form of strength and conditioning training. It is an activity enjoyed by millions the world over in a variety of forms. Body-building, weight-lifting and power-lifting are well developed sports with huge followings in their own right. However, a large percentage of trainees use weight-training for improving various aspects of their general fitness; to develop strength, speed and endurance or a combination of all three. Weight-training routines vary enormously, depending upon the specific aims of the indivdual, and it has proved to be an extremely versatile exercise system. Weights can be used effectively for gaining or losing weight, depending upon the tailoring of training programmes and diet. This makes them doubly attractive to the judoka who may wish to change weight categories while simultaneously improving his physical condition.

Perhaps the most relevant piece of advice for the judoka embarking upon a weight-training programme is to learn the correct exercise technique and to start light and build up gradually. This refers to frequency as well as intensity. Bearing in mind that any weight-training programes undertaken will to some extent conflict with the judoka's chosen activity, it is very important to get the balance of effort right. Whereas a body-builder or power-lifter may train very effectively doing four or five workouts a week with heavy weights, the judoka attempting to emulate such a plan will almost inevitably over-train, although light to medium poundage weights can be used with such frequency if the aim is weight control and endurance. Where heavy weights are being handled on top of hard training in the dojo, two sessions a week is probably ideal, three sessions maximum. In training, as in other aspects of life, more is not always better.

Weight-training can produce rapid improvements in speed, strength and stamina; it can also cause slipped discs and hernias if approached wrongly. The key to progress is correct exercise technique coupled with progressive resistance. The idea of progressive resistance is not a new one. Milo of Croton, a famous strong man living in Ancient Greece in the seventh century BC, was supposed to have acquired his prodigious strength by starting out as a youth carrying a calf around his father's fields. He did this every day, his strength increasing as the animal's weight grew heavier. As the calf turned into a bullock, Milo had to get bigger and stronger in order to be able to carry it until, finally, as a man he was reputed to be capable of carrying a full-grown bull on his shoulders. The tale may well be apocryphal, but it clearly indicates that the Greeks, who inaugurated the Olympic Games and included boxing and wrestling along with athletics, understood the principle of progressive resistance. Modern-day trainers also need to grasp this if they wish to maximize their training efficiency.

People train with weights for a variety of reasons. The body-builder will be concerned primarily with developing muscle mass while keeping body-fat to a minimum in order to display his physique to the best advantage. The Olympic weight-lifter aims to develop the sheer power and athleticism necessary to hoist massive poundages overhead in the clean and jerk or snatch. However, training for such activities is in fact highly specialized, even though it may seem very similar to the uninformed. Even the other major weight-lifting sport of power-lfiting, where the maximum amount of sheer weight that can be shifted at a single attempt in a bench press, squat or dead lift determines who wins, requires a modified training methodology to that used in body-building or weight-lifting. How much more specialized then will be the routines for a combat sport such as judo?

The modern judoka actually falls into the most specialized category of weight-trainer, that of the athlete or sportsman. The sportsman, be he track or field athlete, footballer or rugby player, boxer or skier, will have essentially the same goal: improved sports performance. The judoka is well advised to leave his ego at home when he goes weight-training, as attempting to handle too much weight too soon is courting disaster. Competing with specialist weight-lifters and body-builders and attempting to shift the sort of enormous poundages they can handle is particularly foolish. For such athletes, the training they do with weights is the entirety of their workload and, in many cases, such specialist weight-trainers have been training specifically to lift heavier weights as their sole concern for many years. Everyone who has trained with heavy weights to increase size and power knows that this is half of the process. There is no point in putting your body through arduous, punishing workouts if you do not give it a chance to recover and replenish itself. Some body-builders have been known to take this to extremes, being reluctant to walk anywhere in case they burn off hard-earned muscle mass on the thighs, for instance.

What is true for the international competitor does not apply to the club-level judo player to the same extent. The retired competitor of 3rd dan level or above, who simply enjoys doing judo as a way of keeping fit and exercising, while maintaining some involvement in the sport, may well be so far ahead of the majority of the rest of the players in the club that he will never need to weight-train again. Likewise, a brown belt training three times a week practising judo and planning to enter a grading to get his 1st dan probably does not need to do any weight-training at all. The judo training itself will be sufficient to get him fit and strong enough to win the coveted black belt. There would only be a need to do extra running or weight-training if there were a specific strength or fitness problem. Active dan grades competing at area and national level might need to do supplementary training simply because, as things get closer to national level, that is what the opposition are doing.

In fact, the best way to progress is often to put more effort into the actual judo training, not just in terms of work rate, but in terms of inspiration and imagination, which is where the role of the good coach becomes crucial. Often fighters turn to supplementary conditioning training because they feel their way to progress is blocked, perhaps simply because the opposition is too strong. The way forward lies in assessing needs and implementing strategies to satisfy them. Sometimes this will involve devising a weight-training programme that can be used safely and effectively to make the player more competitive.

The first step before embarking on a weight-training programme to supplement your other training is to define your goals. Why are you going to weight train? Do you want to get faster, stronger, heavier, lighter, fitter or a combination of some of these things? It is a lot easier to get somewhere if you know where you are going. Training specificity has to be considered along with phasing. It is more effective to train for one quality at a time and it is usually best to allocate blocks of time to those things you plan to train for. One popular approach is to spend six weeks concentrating on general endurance – longish runs followed by circuits – then six weeks on local muscular endurance and strength, then six weeks on power training and finally, in the period close to competition, six weeks training for speed and sharpening of techniques, with weights assuming a minor strength-maintenance role, involving maybe one or, at the most two, sessions a week to keep strength levels from deteriorating. Of course, the individual needs to experiment and find out what produces the best results for him personally. The important thing is to strike the right balance of effort and training in the gym and in the dojo.

Naturally, the top-flight international competitor will have hugely different require-ments to the middle-aged club dan grade who aspires not to an Olympic gold but just to being a bit fitter so he can get through sessions, since he finds himself running out of steam towards the end.

Training with maximum poundages in weight-lifting is highly anaerobic. Repetition squats with heavy weights, for instance, are totally gruelling. The body simply cannot supply enough oxygen to keep the muscles working, hence the intense feelings of breathlessness accompanying such an activity. Shuttle runs also produce an anaerobic effect and, for the super fit, can be done with weights held in the hands to put the body under real stress. Such high intensity work should only be done once or, at the most, twice a week, otherwise injury, or at least over-training, will be the likely result.

The following circuit is fairly short in duration, being brief but intense, and is particularly suitable for anyone who wants to weight-train but finds himself pushed for time, because of other commitments. It was devised and popularized by the light heavyweight judo player, David Starbrook, Britain's first Olympic silver medallist in judo, and is effectively a giant set consisting of various exercises performed one after another without any rests. It is best suited to athletes who have done at least three years training in their given sport. It is not something which should be attempted by a novice or anyone who is not already in good physical condition as it is extremely stressful. Anyone uncertain as to their current level of fitness would be well advised to consult a doctor first and then get a fitness check done by a reputable consultant.

This circuit improves strength and fitness and specifically develops the upper body and grip strength, without unduly increasing bulk. In various forms, it can be used to increase stamina, develop strength endurance and lose weight to greater or lesser degrees, depending on what your priorities are. If you want to use it for all the foregoing but also to increase sheer strength, the overload principle has to be employed. More of that later, first let us consider the exercises that comprise the circuit.

The circuit contains eight separate exercises: the military press, the French press, reverse curls, bent-over rowing, curls, step-ups, bent-arm pull-overs and leg raises. They are to be done in that order. Each exercise is performed in a group or set of ten repetitions, except leg raises which are done in sets of thirty. The step-ups entail doing ten repetitions for each leg. These eight exercises are done consecutively, without any rests, using a barbell which is gripped at all times, except when doing the leg raises. The exercises are repeated twice, for a total of three sets.

The tempo of the circuit is fast but good form should still be observed, especially on the bent-over rowing and curls, where there is a tendency to cheat by swinging the weights and getting the back into it when fatigued. For improved strength endurance and cardio-vascular fitness, the circuit should be preceded by a brisk run of between one and a half and three miles. Even if you are trying to lose weight, more than three miles is not recommended as the circuit itself will rapidly deplete any glycogen reserves in the body and if you overdo the running, you will, at best, be too slow at the circuit and, at worst, you will be simply incapable of completing it. Aim to complete the run at a 6 to 8-minute-mile pace (the lighter you are, the faster you should do it), and the circuit itself should take 10 to 12 minutes.

Select a weight equal to about one-third body-weight initially. If you can do it in under 10 minutes, increase the weight by 2k (5lb) until you reach a weight that takes you at least that long to do it. Conversely, if it takes you longer than 12 minutes, the weight is probably too heavy so reduce the weight by 2k (5lb) until you can get it under 12 minutes. When you get the time for the circuit down to 10 minutes, increase the weight by 2k (5lb). This makes a considerable difference to the difficulty of performance of this circuit and bigger jumps will result in a loss of form or possible failure to complete it.

To accelerate weight loss and improve cardio-vascular fitness, a jog after the circuit is suggested. Ideally, this jog should be done immediately after the circuit itself, just as the circuit should immediately follow the initial run. Even a short rest after the run makes it considerably easier to perform and, for an enhanced training effect, all forms of taking a rest should be avoided. The post-circuit jog is initially very hard and breathing is very difficult to control but, if you persevere, you will find you actually recover more quickly by doing the jog, as you get rid of the lactic acid that has built up.

After five or six weeks of doing this, trainees often find themselves able to run rather than jog and literally raring to go as a result of their increased fitness. One of the great pluses of this particular form of training is that it does not cause the chronic stiffness that often seems to indicate that weights are incompatible with judo. To succeed with this circuit training, you must have a positive mental attitude and attack the circuit. The equipment required is very basic, just a set of dumb-bells, a bench and a lot of determination.

Experiment with the circuit; use it as you see fit. Try doing it three, five and even seven days a week, if you are using fairly light weights. Give it at least a month and preferably six weeks but no longer than that. After that time, switch to a different system; you can always return to it at a later date. Some trainees complain of sore lower backs from doing this circuit, usually as a result of failing to observe strict form. If you experience lower back pain, do some back raises (sometimes described as hyper-extensions) but only come up to 180 degrees; do not arch the back. Start with three sets of ten repetitions and build up to three sets of twenty and that should take care of it. If you find you get a sore neck, that is because of the step-ups and can be avoided by padding the bar with foam rubber.

Ideally, you should try to do it in the morning or early afternoon if you intend to train on the mat that evening, as this gives you a certain amount of recovery time. If exceptionally tired in practice, concentrate on *newaza* or perfecting your timing, as throwing techniques will tend to deteriorate when tired, but always keep in mind that this is only temporary, and that when your fitness reaches highly improved levels you will be vastly more effective. If training in this circuit on alternate days to judo training, you should feel increasingly fitter and mat-work should quickly become less stressful for you but so much more for your training partners!

If you are doing the circuit every day and your mat-work is suffering after three or four weeks, try dropping the weight to the original weight you began training with and you will probably be shocked at how relatively easy it seems, which should convince you of your improvement in strength and endurance even though it may not be immediatley apparent on the mat, where you may initially suffer some performance deterioration from tiredness. After six weeks, stop doing the circuit and take a week in which to just practise judo and the strength endurance improvment will be marked.

The circuit described before is an extremely severe form of training, best suited to advanced judoka, but the same principle can be applied for less well-conditioned athletes, using reduced weights, introducing rest periods, even initially reducing the number of sets to two instead of three. There will still be a considerable training effect in a condensed period of time. Aerobic circuit training using weights is far from limited to this one type of training, indeed the possibilities are numerous, the only real limiting factors being facilities, numbers and space.

Motivational Factors

If you are the sort of individual who cannot resist a bit of competition, choose your training partners and competitors carefully.

Ideally, train with partners roughly your equal in terms of strength, weight and motivation. if your goals are the same, then your training is likely to be much more productive. Three is the ideal number for a training group, especially when training with heavy weights and employing movements like the squat and bench press as two can act as spotters while one works, which is a big plus from a safety point of view. More than three people working in a group will tend to slow things down too much as rest periods between sets become very prolonged. If your training partners are friends, as well, the effectiveness of the training often increases since the occasion becomes an enjoyable social event rather than a monotonous hard slog. An added bonus is that trainees in a group tend to be less inclined to fail to turn up as they will be reluctant to let each other down. Such peer group pressure can be just the spur needed to get the slightly lazy trainee away from the TV or stop him going off down to the pub on those occasions when he feels like skipping training.

Fact and Fiction

It is necessary at this point to dispel certain myths about the dangers of weight-training. Many of these myths, despite repeated refutation by top coaches and trainers, prevail even today. The most widespread of these revolve around the notion that weights make you tight and slow you down. Another common criticism is that when you stop doing weight-training, the muscle gained turns to fat. The other great objection from the martial arts world has always been that if you rely on strength you will not be able to develop the necessary technique and skills and, although you may have some early successes, later, when you fight someone just as strong, you will lose through inferior technique. This is a particularly commonly believed notion. The fact is, the stronger and fitter a fighter is, the easier it is to skill train, and many people taking up martial arts and combat sports lack the necessary basic strength to be really effective.

As for weight-training making you muscle-bound, that is demonstrably not the case and again it is a question of making sure that your training is correctly balanced so that your suppleness does not deteriorate. Stretch the whole body for 10 minutes before and after each session and you should find that exactly the opposite happens: you can actually use weight training to improve your flexibility. Such stretching will compensate for any tightening effect that results from heavy weight training; it is simply a question of remembering what you are training for and not neglecting your stretching techniques.

As far as muscle turning to fat goes, that is a physiological impossiblity. What does happen to some individuals is that they stop training completely and take no pains to modify their diet, in many cases eating and drinking more than when they were training. The unexercised muscle then begins to atrophy and shrink and fat deposits begin to occur all over the body. This is accelerated by inactivity as the body's metabolic rate slows down and less and less calories get burned up in daily life and are stored as fat. Standardized body-building programmes are only really suitable for fighters if their overriding concern is to put on muscular weight. This necessitates a competition-free period of at least six months in which to concentrate exclusively on that, and includes attention to those aspects of body-building that take place outside the gym such as nutrition and recuperation.

Unfortunately, in spite of the proliferation of gymnasiums, health clubs and fitness centres, there is a definite shortage of knowledgeable coaching and direction on the subject of specialized weight-training for improved sports performance. The good coach will make it his business not to become an expert exercise coach, but to get access to someone who is. The judo coach should stick to teaching judo unless, of course, he is also a specialist in exercise physiology. This is one of the major problems the fighter who has no guidance encounters when he goes to a gym and asks for a training programme. The instructors are almost invariably body-builders or physical education teachers. Such people, while generally very knowledgeable, even expert, in their specialized fields generally have little understanding of what training in a combat sport entails.

A weight-training programme for any combat sport has to be a balanced programme that takes into account the particular individual's workload in its entirety, it has to accommodate and complement his other training, not replace or conflict with it. In addition, despite being based upon scientific principles there is a great deal of conflicting information about what is effective and ineffective, safe or unsafe.

Scientists and coaches, weight-trainers and weight-lifters, body-builders and sportsmen, all agree and disagree when it comes to the subject of strength training. Sources of information contradict one another in many important aspects. Certain aspects are the subject of interminable disagreement. The full, deep squat, for instance, is condemned by many authorites on the subject as being a dangerous exercise likely to cause damage to the knees and lower back and therefore to be avoided like the plague. However, other equally authoritative sources regard it as the absolute bedrock of any strength training or bulk building programme, a highly productive if not indispensable exercise which simply has to be done to make any real progress.

A similar situation exists with regard to the bench press, power clean and dead-lift and the individual faced with choosing which exercises to include in his workouts can end up thoroughly confused by it all. Ultimately, the only way to determine an exercise's suitability is to try it and see what effects it has on you. The rules are mutable. Training that makes one person flourish will wither another. However, it is fair to say that anyone who already has knee problems should not do full squats as there is an exceptionally strong probability that the exercise will aggravate the injury. Likewise anyone with back problems should be aware of the dangers inherent in heavy power cleans, squats and dead-lifts. On the other hand, the sensible use of these exercises along with certain assistance exercises can clearly strengthen weak injury-prone areas, so it is really a matter for individual assessment and experiment. To put it another way, if it feels good, do it! Any trial periods ought to allow about three months for an effective assessment of an exercise's suitability.

Correct technique when training with weights is of paramount importance if steady progress is to be made without injury. Equally important is mental flexiblity and the ability to adapt your training to your circumstances. Listen to your body at all times and do not attempt to put unrealistic demands upon it; injury can be avoided if it can be anticipated. If you suffered a knock in training, or a kick in the thigh or a jarred shoulder doing judo the night before it would be total folly to go into the gym the following day and attempt a personal best in the squat or bench press. Regularly attempting personal-best lifts is in fact inherently dangerous and many coaches argue that maximum single-repetition lifts are not worth the effort. A maximum single can be a great confidence builder and increasing your personal best in the bench press from three hundred to three hundred and thirty pounds in three months undoubtedly reinforces faith in the effectiveness of your training, but the maximum single ought not to be attempted every session; it demonstrates strength rather than develops it.

As a general guide, if you cannot do three repetitions with a weight it is too heavy to be useful as a training weight. The important thing to bear in mind is that one huge maximum effort at lifting a weight has very little relevance to your actual sport. If you are not a power-lifter, it is not worth the risk. Of course an occasional attempt at a personal best is necessary to effectively determine current strength levels or assess the extent of improvment in a particular area. On such

occasions you should feel fresh and ready to go and always observe strictly correct exercise form. Attempting a maximum poundage when particularly fatigued is definitely not recommended.

Another important aspect of injury avoidance is the warm up. Going into a gym and lifting heavy weights straight away is dangerous and foolish. Some body-builders promote an approach they tend to label high intensity, but which is inherently dangreous from an injury point of view and psychologically almost impossible to sustain, physically as well if steroids are not being used. Ten minutes warming up with some stretching, skipping, a few minutes on an exercise bike or some callisthenics is the right approach. However, be careful not to burn up all your energy in warming up, especially if you are training for power when you need to be reasonably fresh.

The Set System
Just as repetition is at the heart of training methodology in all the martial arts, so it is in weight-training. Basically, in a weight-training session the amount of work that is to be done is broken up into sets of repetitions. Say, for example, a trainee wanted to do thirty repetitions of the bench press. Using only 100lb he could probably do so in one set of thirty repetitions. However, the result of doing this would be of little value for developing strength since the weight would be too light and would have only an endurance effect on the muscles. Increasing the weight to 70k (150lb), he would find it was probably necessary to stop after ten repetitions and give the muscles a rest before continuing, in which case he might do three sets of ten, with about a minute's rest between sets. If he chose to increase the weight to 80k (180lb), he might find he could only do five repetitions, in which case to achieve his original target of thirty repetitions he would need to do six sets. Taking the principle still further, ten sets of three with 90k (200lb) would be the logical conclu-

sion. Although the total number of repetitions is the same, the workload has doubled from the first workout.

This illustrates the principle and value of training in sets, since they allow heavier weights to be handled with consequent increases in strength, speed and power being made possible which would otherwise not be feasible. Of course, how many repetitions you can do with a given weight is determined by how strong you are and the poundage being handled.

Determining what poundage to train with depends upon what you are training for and recent Soviet research into the prerequisites of strength training has interesting implications for the combat sportsman. To put it simply, the belief among Russian strength coaches, who have produced some of the strongest men in the world, is that training affects the trainee in the following ways:

1. Training with less than 50 per cent of your maximum will only develop stamina and not absolute strength as the training action will invariably be too ballistic.
2. Training with weights that range from 50–80 per cent of your maximum primarily develops speed.
3. Training with weights that range from 80–95 per cent of your maximum develops speed in conjunction with strength.
4. Training with weights of 95 per cent of your maximum develops strength only.

These maximums refer to the maximum poundage that can be handled for one repetition. Therefore, a power-lifter capable of a single 180k (400lb) bench press, wanting to train at 95 per cent of his maximum would have to lift 170k (380lb). Conseqently he would, at least once a week initially, need to do ten sets of three, since it is highly unlikely that he could do more repetitions with such a heavy weight. It is no great cognitive leap to infer from this that the different needs of judo players require quite different approaches.

The figher training with weights to supplement his aerobic work and speed up weight loss should train in the 50–80 per cent range, whereas the judoka attempting to develop an effective *ura-nage* (a pick-up throw requiring considerable explosive strength and co-ordination) ought to work in the 80–95 per cent range.

The apparently arbitrary nature of the number of sets and repetitions to be performed is pretty well established according to physiological responses to exercise and determined by working out the trainee's current absolute maximum in a given lift and then allocating a workload which is a percentage of that maximum. The number of repetitions done and the weight to be used are then calculated bearing in mind the functions of the training percentages listed above; 6 x 6 is common as a power-building routine, whereas 3 x 10 is normally appropriate to those training mainly to improve speed and strength endurance. Howver, bear in mind that the importance of the number of repetitions and sets is determined by the poundage as a percentage of your maximum. Muscle tone will improve to some extent whichever system is employed. Of course, the same methodology has to be applied to a whole group of exercises, since only doing one exercise would be of little value. A typical workout would then comprise eight to twelve different exercises for the various muscle groups in order to have a whole body training effect.

More Pre-Training Considerations

The only real objection to the novice judoka weight-training is that, given the rigorous demands of judo, weight-training on top might result in over-training. However, it can be recommended in off season, or when other demands prevent regular training in the dojo, as an alternative to losing condition. The ratio of weight-training sessions to actual dojo workouts has to be determined by need. A really weak, unfit judo player, for instance, might be better off doing weights three times a week and judo only twice until he felt himself to be physically strong enough to compete in the dojo on more equal terms. Then he could switch to three judo sessions and reduce the weight-training to twice a week to maintain his strength gains. However, a very strong fighter would be better advised to make good use of his strength by skill training and trying to develop the speed of his techniques, perhaps only doing weights once a week to maintain and monitor strength levels.

The use of heavy poundages without adequate foundation training can certainly be counter-productive. Heavy squats and power cleans can cause chronic musclar soreness if you try too much too soon and will undoubtedly cause a deterioration in your actual performance on the mat. Attempting to practise or fight with any intensity in such a tired state is folly and an open invitation to injury. The rational way to proceed is to start with moderate poundages and build up gradually.

Appendix I

The History of Judo in the West

by George Kerr

The history of judo in the West is a fascinating tale, but some understanding of its genesis in Japan is crucial to an awareness of why many of the issues and structures of the modern activity came into being. Over a century has passed since Jigoro Kano founded the original Kodokan in February 1882 and that original judo club (literally the place for studying the way), has expanded from some ten individuals practising on eight *tatami* – straw mats measuring 6ft (2m) by 3ft (1m) – into a truly multi-national organization, under the auspices of the International Judo Federation with an estimated 10,000,000 practitioners world wide. This phenomenal growth in just over a century is testament to the remarkable achievement of Dr Kano and his followers as well as the inherent appeal and value of judo as an activity.

Jigoro Kano was a remarkable man in many ways. His fascination with ju jitsu and judo stemmed from having been a weak and sometimes sickly child who soon discovered one of the harsh realities of existence: that the strong tend to prey on the weak. As a child, he took up a variety of sports with the aim of getting stronger and conditioning himself so that he would be able to stand up against bullies and the like. He discovered in ju jitsu a means to combine a number of personal interests and requirements. The principal forms of ju jitsu that he studied were Kito ryu and Tenjin Shin'yo ryu and from his studies he derived his own system of judo based on the principle of the maximum efficient use of mental and physical energy.

The two ju-jitsu ryu in which Kano studied were not sporting clubs, but dojo where martial arts practice took place. The majority of training took the form of *kata*, although there is evidence that students were familiar with another method of practice called *nokori-ai*, which had begun to be used shortly before the Meji restoration in 1868. *Nokori-ai* was a modified type of *kata* training which was the precursor of modern-style *randori*. Partners would practise a set of techniques, just as in the *kata*, but if tori (the thrower) did an ineffective technique, uke might apply a counter throw. If tori were able to, he would then attempt to counter uke's counter. Kano was an innovator and saw in this practice the potential for a more apposite and rewarding form of training, but still intended to train the student in attack and defense in keeping with the ethos of the original martial arts. Kano named his new form of training *randori* (free play) and, in his master text *Kodokan Judo*, has this to say about it.

'*Randori* means "free practice". Partners pair off and vie with each other in an actual match. They may throw, pin, choke and apply joint locks, but they may not hit, kick or employ other techniques appropriate only to actual combat. The main conditions in *randori* are that participants take care not to injure each other and that they follow judo etiquette, which is mandatory if one is to derive the maximum benefit from *randori*. Randori may be practised either as training in the methods of attack and defense or as physical education. In either case, all movements are made in conformity with the principle of maximum efficiency. If training in attack and defence is the objective, concentration on the proper execution of techniques is sufficient. But beyond that, *randori* is ideal for physical culture since it involves all parts of the body and, unlike gymnastics, all its movements are purposeful and executed with spirit. The objective of this systematic physical training is to perfect control over mind and body and to prepare a person to meet any emergency or attack, accidental or intentional.'

This authoritative definition of *randori* makes an interesting text for consideration in the light of the kind of motivation evident amongst the modern-day practitioners of judo, whose obsession with winning and not being beaten would seem to override all other concerns. Judo was designed to be training for mind, body and character and all that was learned within it was intended to be applied to living a better life. Competition was of minor importance:

'Contests in judo have as their rationale the idea that the lessons taught in matches will find application not only in future training, but in the world at large.' Judo was conceived then as training for life, not as a replacemnt for it as many young sportsmen would seem to want it to be. I believe in the value of judo as training and am an elitist in my attitude to life as indeed Kano was. I believe in success and that it should be rewarded and probably have an American or indeed Japanese attitude to success, despite being Scots. In Japan, the players who reach a high level and honour their country by winning world and Olympic medals are looked after by the system, they are not professional in the western sense of the word, but they are taken care of (al-

though, not to the same extent as the Koreans who, for winning an Olympic gold medal, are guaranteed an annual salary for life the equivalent to what they might earn in a decent job quite apart from whatever else they might earn elsewhere after deciding what to do with their lives after competition!) Many Japanese competitors move on from competition into teaching and coaching, all paid positions, which contasts sharply with what happens in the West. In fact, it is difficult to speak of judo in the West in this context as there is such a variety of current practice from country to country. The French perhaps lead the way in Europe in terms of marketing and development of professionalism within the sport, which is unsurprising as they have the best organized and wealthiest federation in Europe. The French Federation was the driving force behind the 1988 Paris prize-fight when big money prizes were offered to top fighters. Jean-Luc Rouge believes that the morale and self-esteem of today's top judo players demands that they have the same financial inducements and career opportunities as other top sportsmen and women. To a certain extent, his position echoes Sato's question about why the Japanese child should do judo when he can play baseball. If top western judo athletes do not have the same opportunites as their peers in other sports, such as athletics, golf, tennis and boxing, where vastly greater sums of money are meted out, then what is there to keep them in the sport of judo? Perhaps, more importantly what is there about the sport of judo to inspire the youth of today to want to be the champions of tomorrow. We live in a capitalist society and success equates with wealth. The Olympic judo champion who cannot afford a car to take him to and from training will be regarded as little more than an interesting eccentric, rather than an inspirational role model. The modern youngster with a leaning towards combat sports will tend to be much more impressed and consequently inclined to emulate the relatively wealthy karate instructor with the flashy sports car than the judo teacher who rides home on his bicycle. This may be unfortunate and even sad, but it is reality and has to be confronted, the time has passed for burying our heads in the sand.

The top French competitors are professionals in all but name and no secret is made of the payments that they receive. The FFJDA get around the rules by insisting that players are true amateurs in the way that top athletes in Britain are allowed to be, with payments being made to trust funds and loans being granted in lieu of guaranteed future income. All the promising youngsters who train in the French system tend to go and live in Paris and the best of them are looked after, being given sinecures to fund their training. Many have jobs they never go to and are effectively paid while they train. Judo in France is better organized and has far better media coverage, especially on television, than anyone outside of Japan. As a consequence, judo in France is better financed and has more kudos than anywhere else in Europe. There are also more license holders, all of whom pay monies to their federation, which is an interesting correlation that should be noted by all those concerned with the development of the sport in other countries.

Other countries have to learn from the French where possible. Those individuals involved with the governing bodies of judo in each country have to consider how to breed success, from the grass roots promotion in judo – getting more members, constructing more purpose-built dojos, developing media relations and effective marketing strategies – to producing top-class internationals who function as flagships that represent the country abroad.

Many conservatives who occupy positions of power in the organisational bureaucracy are guilty of severely undervaluing the players themselves, almost as much as the players undervalue the officials who make the events they participate in possible. How could there b a World Championships without organ-

izers, timekeepers, referees, etc? Equally important, how could there be one without competitors? The top players have the potential to be the sport's most marketable commodity and its biggest attraction. They are the role models that the sport offers to the parents of the youngsters who need an outlet for their boundless physical energy. It is vitally important that they feel rewarded for their effort. It is equally important that they learn to present themselves professionally and effectively. If they cannot do this, they must be taught to do so. This may be considered as another of the educational aspects of judo.

Many international champions have to go down this road and find it to be almost as hard as the contest trail because it requires a willingness to learn and a great capacity to adapt. My number one protégé, Peter Seisenbacher, is a case in point. When he won the Olympic gold medal in 1984, he became Austria's first gold medallist in living memory. He was voted sports personality of the year and was thrust centre stage by the media, the eyes of his nation were upon him. It fell to me to educate him not just in judo but in the social skills needed to prepare him to cope with his success. He had to learn just as much off the mat as on it and sometimes the adjustments that it was necessary to make were very great indeed. However, I was in the position of having gone through the same kind of educational process, thanks to my time spent with Mr Leggett. Therefore, life repeats itself and, just as I made a success of my life by setting up and running the Edinburgh club, so Peter now occupies the number two position in Austrian sport, reporting directly to the Minister for Sport. I know the value of a proper social education from experience and the difficulties it represents for someone who is basically a fighter, but I also know that the instruction and training received in judo stand you in very good stead for learning the lessons necessary for a successful life outside the dojo. Now too, does Peter Seisenbacher.

Even in Britain, money can be made available to successful players in the form of allowances for training expenses and grants, but many young men make the mistake of going on the dole in order to train full time. While such dedication and apparent self-sacrifice may seem laudable to some, the consequences are rarely very satisfying. The lack of real income, low self-esteem and social deprecation that go with this situation means that most operate from a basis of extremely low morale and are rarely able to perform as well as they might. Such young men and women would be better off going into further or higher education or aiming to develop careers that will allow them to have a parallel judo career. Such a very small number actually make it in judo that the decision to sacrifice their potential for other achievements is misplaced and the practice should be discouraged.

All of this is a far cry from Kano's original perception of judo. It was actually never Kano's intention that judo be practised by anyone and everyone. He envisaged it as a spiritual discipline for the attainment of self-perfection. However, he was the son of an influential and affluent upper-middle-class merchant family and unquestioningly accepted the higher moral values of his class. Therefore, he was quite discriminating over who he would and who he would not teach. He envisaged judo very much as an activity to be enjoyed by a social elite, continually refining themselves spiritually through practice, and hoped that in this way it could make a genuine contribution to world-wide understanding and pave the way for peace.

Judo in the twentieth century is really judo for all, anyone and everyone is encouraged to participate. This popularization was the price that had to be paid for judo to be accepted as a sport by the western world. Whether it has contributed significantly to world peace is impossible to judge, but it has certainly helped promote mutual respect and understanding at the very least on an indivdiual basis among those who have trained and fought together.

Friendliness between sporting rivals, particularly after the event, is not unusual but the peculiarly intimate nature of the judo contest, in common with boxing, seems to go deeper than most sports. Many old foes end up being life-long friends, even if they are nationals of different countries.

Whether or not all of Kano's achievements can be attributed to his passion for judo is debatable, but they are by any standards impressive. He was born in Hyogo prefecture in 1860 and founded the Kodokan at the tender age of twenty-two, a year after graduating from Tokyo University with a degree in literature, politics and political economy. An educationalist by choice, he became a high school principal early in his career and later principal of the prestigious Tokyo Higher Normal School. In 1889, as a member of the Imperial Household Department, he made a study tour of European educational establishments and, twenty years later, became the first Japanese member of the International Olympic Committee. He was also founder president of the Japan Amateur Sports Association in 1911. In 1922, he was elected to the House of Peers (the Japanese equivalent to becoming a member of the House of Lords) and lived a fruitful and productive life until 1938 when he died at sea, aboard the Hikawa Maru, while returning from an IOC meeting in Cairo. As a role model, he takes some beating, but the latter part of Kano's life was in good part spent addressing the issue of the sportification of judo. Having founded something unique, the great dilemma for him was how to popularize it without selling it short as a mere sport. However, the western world in particular seemed to value it most highly in that guise and that is something that has not changed.

THE ORIGINS OF JUDO IN BRITAIN

The British general public's first encounters with judo in England came by way of ju jitsu performances in the country's music halls. Before the advent of the cinema, and later television, the music halls were the major source of entertainment. In the late nineteenth and early twentieth century, prior to the global domination via the mass media now so familiar to us, all the acts were live. Singers, magic acts, strong men, dancers, comedians and even well known sporting personalities, frequently stepped up on stage for the appreciation of a fee-paying public. Performers included boxers and wrestlers, some of them the world champions of the day.

It was an Englishman, William Barton-Wright, who brought ju jitsu to England, arranging demonstrations and challenge matches in music halls up and down the country. A civil engineer by profession, but independently wealthy, Barton-Wright had studied ju jitsu with Jigoro Kano in Japan and, on his return to England, founded his own self-defence system, naming it *Bartitsu*.

In an effort to publicize and market his system, he imported two Japanese experts, the Tani brothers, in 1899, with whom he toured the music halls, challenging all comers. One of the brothers quickly grew homesick and returned to Japan after only a few months; the other, Yukio Tani, remained and became a legend in his own lifetime, as well as very wealthy. Tani, who was no more than 5ft 4in tall, performed with another fairly small Japanese, S.K. Uyenshi, touring the country and taking on all comers, including boxers, wrestlers, street fighters and drunks. Few of their opponents were trained professional fighters, but the rewards offered for beating either of the pair were high. Anyone staying on their feet for fifteen minutes could earn £20, the equivalent of 10 week's wages for the average working man. The key to the ju jitsu men's success was that they insisted that all their opponents dress in the unfamiliar jacket and belt, which gave them the advantage they needed, especially when they came up against skilful wrestlers. Tani's most difficult bout was against a wrestler, James Mellor, reputedly the world lightweight catch-as-catch can champion, whom he had to fight, because of a promoter's boast, without wearing the jackets. Tani won by two falls to one after a bout lasting an hour, giving some indication of his level of ability, although he often said there were many better than himself in Japan.

This proved to be true and Tani was eventually discredited when he was effectively taken apart in 1905 by another ju jitsu expert, Taro Miyake, the 1904 All Japan Champion. Tani had separated from Barton-White and had a new manager in William Bankier, but Tani's ex-manager, eager to discredit him and establish a new expert, had arranged for Miyake to come over from Japan. The younger, fitter Miyake was in top form and wiped the floor with Tani, destroying the myth of his invincibility that had made him so popular for so long. Ultimately, no one involved benefited from this because destroying the myth of Tani's invincibility also more or less ended ju jitsu's music hall appeal. Various nomadic ju jitsu men sporadically turned up from Japan to make the rounds, none achieved the fame, notoriety and, indeed, wealth enjoyed by Tani in his heyday. However, ju jitsu clubs did spring up as a result of all the publicity, and self-defence courses for ladies abounded.

THE BUDOKWAI

The very next year saw the arrival in Britain of one of the key figures in the history of British judo, Gunji Koizumi, who was to found what is now the oldest judo club in Europe, the Budokwai, in London, which opened in 1918 as the Budokwai Ju-Jitsu School. The use of the term ju-jitsu is evidence to the notoriety of Tani and the other Japanese exponents and the considerable benefits that their escapades had in publicizing and promoting the infant judo movement. This was certainly not something that Japan's judo establishment had any part in coordinating, in fact it was in direct contravention of Kodokan rules laid down by Dr Kano himself which expressly forbid performances of judo for profit or using judo skills outside of the dojo. At the club's first practice on 26 January 1918 there were about 30 or 40 people on the mat, but all were Japanese. Much of the training was traditional ju-jitsu, not Kodokan judo, and, in fact, it was not until Kano himself visited the club in 1921 that it became affiliated to the Kodokan, and Koizumi and his chief instructor, Yukio Tani, were awarded Kodokan grades in recognition of their ability and achievements. The early history of the Budokwai is really the early history of British and indeed European judo, preceding as it did both the BJA and the EJU.

During the first decade before the war, the dojo in Lower Grosvenor Place was host to some of the now legendary figures in the judo movement, including Kano himself, Nagaoka and Kotani, the only surviving 10th dan. Kano and Nagaoka, when they visited Britain as part of a world tour to promote Kodokan judo, started the British Yudanshakai. One of the first occidental students was Marcus Kaye who later became president of the Budokwai and who was to be T.P. Leggett's instructor when he came along in the 1930s. At one point, the Budokwai was actually a branch of the Kodokan, although the connections were suspended at the outbreak of the Second World War. Nevertheless, it was significant that when T.P. Leggett, who worked for the British Embassy in Tokyo was interned, he was permitted to practise judo with his guards.

After the war, he returned to London and the Budokwai to pave the way for a whole succession of Japanese instructors. The first of these was Mr Kawamura, a big man, who came over in the early 1950s. He was ably assisted by Mr Nishimura and Mr Nakanishi and it was these men who were largely responsible for the quality judoka produced who represented Britain in the late 1950s and who won the European Championhips three times in succession. The late 1950s saw the arrival of Mr Saburo Matsushita and then, in the early 1960s one of the most spectacular judo men of the post-war period, Kisaburo Watanabe, who had such a profound influence on the top contest men of the 1960s and early 1970s, such as Jacks, Parisi and, to a lesser extent, Starbrook.

A similar pattern was being repeated in various European countries with varying degrees of success. Japanese high-grade judo men were arriving, setting up clubs and teaching their art to the French, Germans, Italians, Dutch and indeed any who wanted to learn. One European, in particular, was learning the ropes in the mid to late 1950s and was to have the most profound effect on Japanese, and in turn world, judo: Holland's Anton Geesink. Geesink was a giant of a man, six feet six inches tall and very athletically built; he weighed about 270–80lb with very little fat. He was to become European Champion twenty times, World Champion twice and, perhaps most significantly, Olympic Champion in the 1964 Olympic Games in Tokyo, humbling the best the Japanese had to offer on their own home ground. Geesink's skill was formidable. In the 1961 World Championship, when he won the title for the first time, he showed a wide range of throwing and *newaza* skills, in order to defeat each of his opponents in turn by ippon. He threw his first opponent, an Indonesian, for ippon with *osoto-gari*, the second, Bourgoine of France, with *sasae-tsuri-komi-ashi*, the third, Kaminaga, for two *waza-aris* with *okuri-ashi-barai*, the fourth, a Yugoslav, with *okuri-ashi-barai*, and Koga of Japan, in the semifinal, with *uchimata*. In the final against the World Champion, Sone, Geesink's superior physical power and size were obvious, but so too were his technical and strategic ability. He dominated the Japanese from the start, completely out-gripping him. He soon got ahead by scoring *waza-ari* with *osoto-makikomi* and then made a very adept *tani-otoshi-kaeshi-waza* to a Sone attack to take him to the ground and hold him in an inescapable *mune-gatame*. Three years later he devastated the Japanese judo world by defeating Akio Kaminaga in the Olympic final, throwing him with *sasae-tsuri-komi-ashi* in the preliminaries and holding him with *kesa-gatame* for ippon.

One of the secrets of Geesink's succss was that he would go to Japan for three-month spells and train there, then return to Europe to consolidate what he had learned there and concentrate on improving his physical condition specifically for big events. As well as possessing obvious physical advantages, Geesink was clever too and earned every possible psychological advantage that he could. One story tells of how he found out where and when the Japanese Olympic team went running in the mornings. He made a point of going there an hour before them every morning for a week, so that as they were going out to run they would see him coming back already sweating profusely and glowing with fitness after his morning running, while they were still bleary-eyed. Then, while they spent the rest of the morning worrying about how hard he must be training he would go back to bed to catch up on his sleep so that he would be fresh for *randori* and *newaza* later in the day.

It was one of the biggest disappointments of my life that I did not represent Great Britain at the Tokyo Olympic Games. The best years of my competitive judo career spanned 1961–64. In 1964, I took the silver medal in the European Championships at open weight behind Geesink and was confident that, with a little luck, I could win an Olympic medal. However, at that time, I was working full time, managing the Renshuden, and when the Olympic trials were held my entry was refused by Mr Charles Palmer on the grounds that my amateur status was questionable. Three weeks after the trials, I was able to produce a letter from Sir Arthur Gold of the British Olympic Committee confirming my eligibility, but it was too late and so to no avail. It was a typical example of the confusion between professional and amateur status that continues to dog judo even to this day.

Geesink shattered the myth of Japanese invincibility, but over the years they have tried pretty hard to re-establish it. The battle between them and the rest of the world has gone to and fro many times, but there have been some major shocks for them at various moments in the history of the sport. One of the most dramatic was the emergence of the Soviet Union as a force to be reckoned with when Olympic recognition for the sport became a reality. With their strong tradition in Sombo wrestling, a form of wrestling wearing jackets very similar to the judo garb, but allowing leglocks as well, with many of the various throwing techniques found in judo, they had little difficulty in adapting to the different rule structure of judo. They changed judo as dramatically as the contraceptive pill altered society. They were fearless fighters with little or no respect for the Japanese, whom most Europeans still held in awe; they had no regard for reputation and caused some major upsets. Isao Okano himself, one of the all-time great champions was humiliated by being armlocked at a time when he was reigning All-Japan Champion. In typical samurai style, he had refused to submit to the technique until his elbow was badly damaged. The shame and loss of face were far more damaging to him though it is said that for six months after his defeat (the first ever to a foreigner) he did not leave his house. This was no mere post-defeat depression but a life or death situation. Fortunately, the true judo spirit asserted itself and Okano came back to win the 1965 world title.

Sombo has no strangles, but what it did allow were armlocks, and the Russians wreaked absolute havoc with their clinically efficient *juji-gatames*, sometimes brought off from the standing position! Their judo was characterized by its unorthodox flavour but they had many fighters with good, strong *koshi-waza* (hip techniques), frequently performed by taking an initial grip on the opponent's belt, and had considerable success in the early years with their specialized version of *ura-nage*, which they imported from sombo.

THE SPREAD OF JUDO IN THE WEST

Following the emergence of the Russians as a force to be reckoned with in international judo, the trend has been towards a gradual sharing of success among the European countries, with an increasing number of the world's nations sharing out the honours in international tournaments, generally at the expense of the Japanese. Countries such as Poland, Brazil, Egypt, Mongolia and the USA have all managed to produce top international competitors who have won medals at world and olympic level, and the trend continues. African judo looks set to emerge as yet another force in the last decade of the twentieth century. The Chinese are back in international competition and beginning to make their presence felt. The future looks very interesting. There have also been some surprising developments, such as the introduction of blue judo suits for the purpose of making the televizing of judo easier and more attractive, which was anathema to the conservative judo establishment in Japan when Isao Okano suggested it some two decades ago. The realization of this change in the appearance of judo is attributable to European influence and Anton Geesink, in particular, who lobbied forcefully to have it implemented. The blue suits were first used officially, with great success, at the 1988 European Championships in Pamplona in Spain. They have not yet been accepted at the World Championships and the Olympic Games but it is possible that this may yet come about. With the massive developments that have occurred in women's judo, which has finally achieved full Olympic status for the 1992 Games in Barcelona, there are already double the number of competitors to keep track of! Anything which helps distinguish the competitors from one another ought to be helpful.

The great general advantage the Japanese have is their strength in depth, while the West continue to produce great individual champions such as Rouge, van de Walle, Adams, Parisi and Seisenbacher, these men represent the tip of what might be described as a needle pyramid. The Japanese have a much bigger pyramid and it has a much broader skill base.

The future for judo in the West relies on grass roots enthusiasm from a hard core of amateurs who embody the traditional judo values of never giving up and of doing everything in a sincere way. It also relies upon professional management within the governing bodies and federations. The management of something which has grown so big and is now so important to so many people ought not to be left to chance. The people who interact to run the various national and international federations need to develop mutual self-respect. This is the only basis for professional management and is particularly important where powerful dominating personalities are concerned. · Without professional management, it is unlikely that the judo movement will be able to steer the course it needs to follow to continue to thrive and grow in the twenty-first century.

Appendix II

World Championships and Olympic Games:

Results and Analysis by Peter Seisenbacher

The following lists of results are intended for reference and are really for the student of the history of judo contest. They provide all the necessary information for making statistical comparisons of the progress or otherwise of the world's judo nations in international competition at the highest level. They are also useful for those who enjoy following the progress of particular fighters from year to year. They make particularly interesting comparison with results for European Championships of the same period; unfortunately space does not permit the inclusion of those too.

The results from the Olympic Games of 1980 and 1984 are a little unrepresentative of the true state of world judo as the Japanese were absent from the former event and the Russians from the latter as a result of politically based boycotts. This is unfortunate but judo was not the only sport to suffer from these boycotts.

The only attempt ever made to politically sabotage a World Judo Championships took place in 1977 when they were due to be held in Barcelona in Spain. The culprits were China and Spain. China was exercising her considerable diplomatic muscle in order to isolate Taiwan (formerly Formosa and now Taipei) and the Spanish government were unwilling to issue visas for the Taiwan contingent despite having promised to do so for all IJF members. Two weeks before the event was due to take place it was summarily cancelled. This was a drastic course of action, but

the IJF and the IOC and Mr Charles Palmer, the then president of the IJF were really left with no choice. The judo world was disappointed at the time but since that event there have been no further efforts to use judo for political motives as happens so often in other sports and no subseqent championships have been disrupted. It would seem that the course of action taken was the right one.

The general tendency when considering the medal statistics is to analyse them in terms of Japan against the rest, but it is equally valuable to compare the relative successes of individual countries and competitors, a lot can be gleaned about individual character and personality from such considerations. For instance, who would have thought that Poland's perennial bronze medallist Pawlowski, who won bronzes in the European Championships in 1982, 1983 and 1986, would defeat the reigning Japanese World Champion Yamamoto in the semifinals of the Olympic games in Seoul in 1988 in the under 65k class, 9 years after winning his first and only other major medal, a bronze at the 1979 Paris World Championships? In the semifinal, he was trailing the Japanese by koka, yuko and waza-ari with less than 30 seconds to go when he threw him for ippon with a totally unexpected *ippon seoi-nage*. He went on to lose in the final, but an Olympic silver medal in the twilight of his career in the lightwight class was totally unexpected. Kashiwazaki of Japan, who took silver in the

Fig 81 The ability to adapt is crucial to success in modern judo. An unidentified French fighter scores spectacularly here with a *kata-gurama* follow-up to a *seoi-nage* attack.

1975 World Championships, had to wait six years for a second chance, which he got when he finally won his gold medal in Maastricht in 1981. His countryman, Shozo Fuji, was four times World Champion, and yet never picked to represent Japan in an Olympic Games. These men have passed into judo legend along with the truly famous, the Geesinks and the Ruskas, the Yamashitas and the Okanos. We owe it to judo to remember them and keep their stories alive. There are many such tales hidden beneath the black and white of the statistics, human sagas, stories of hardship and struggle, triumph and defeat, elation and disappointment, but most of all of the enduring judo spirit is their mute witness to the qualities of dedication and determination that produce champions. The pursuit of excellence it seems need not be inimical to the quest for self-perfection, despite all the argument to the contrary.

The implications for the future are especially interesting as we enter the last decade of the twentieth century and social and political change and upheaval is accelerating across the world. The changes in the socialist systems of Eastern Europe into free market economies, together with the reunification of the two Germanys, may have considerable significance for the future of judo. At the time of writing, such social disorder can only favour a turn of the wheel back to the Japanese,

Fig 82 Katsuhiko Kashiwazaki of Japan throws Torsten Reisman of East Germany for ippon with *uchimata sukashi* on the way to the world title in the u65k category in 1981, in Maastricht, Holland.

although perhaps the old analogy with the hungry men making the best fighters may once again prove to be true and we may see a whole new generation of tough Eastern Europeans trying to fight their way out of obscurity and poverty through judo. Another factor to consider is how much the African nations will improve over the next decade. Although conspicuously absent from World Championship judo, they have grown noticeably in stature when they participate in events like the Olympics. Perhaps the next decade will see an even greater levelling of ability and sharing out of medals than happened in the 1988 Olympics? Perhaps, too, financial and economic success has made the Japanese soft and we shall never see the likes of Okano and Yamashita again. As we stand on the threshhold of a new century the prospects look exciting for judo. Who knows what the future might hold?

WORLD CHAMPIONSHIPS

Men's 1st World Judo Championships, Tokyo, Japan, 1956

Category		Name	Country
Open	1	Matsui	Japan
	2	Yoshimatsu	Japan
	3	Geesink	Netherlands
	3	Courtine	France

Men's 2nd World Judo Championships, Tokyo, Japan, 1956

Category		Name	Country
Open	1	Sone	Japan
	2	Kaminaga	Japan
	3	Yamashki	Japan
	3	Pariset	France

Men's 3rd World Judo Championships, Paris, France, 1961

Category		Name	Country
Open	1	Geesink	Netherlands
	2	Sone	Japan
	3	Koga	Japan
	3	Kim	South Korea

Men's 4th World Judo Championships, Rio de Janeiro, Brazil, 1965

Category		Name	Country
u68k	1	Matsuda	Japan
	2	Minatoya	Japan
	3	Stepanov	USSR
	3	Park	South Korea
u80k	1	Okano	Japan
	2	Yamanaka	Japan
	3	Kim	South Korea
	3	Bregman	USA
o80k	1	Geesink	Netherlands
	2	Matsunaga	Japan
	3	Sakaguchi	Japan
	3	Rogers	Canada
Open	1	Inokuma	Japan
	2	Kibrosachvilli	USSR
	3	Snijders	Netherlands
	3	Kiknadze	USSR

Men's 5th World Judo Championships, Salt Lake City, USA, 1967

Category		Name	Country
u63k	1	Shigeoka	Japan
	2	Matsuda	Japan
	3	Suslin	USSR
	3	Kim	South Korea
u70k	1	Minatoya	Japan
	2	Park S.	South Korea
	3	Nakatani	Japan
	3	Park C.	South Korea
u80k	1	Maruki	Japan
	2	Poglagen	Netherlands
	3	Enju	Japan
	3	Jacks	Great Britain
u93k	1	Sato N.	Japan
	2	Sato O.	Japan
	3	Eugster	Netherlands
	3	Herrmann	West Germany
o93k	1	Ruska	Netherlands
	2	Maejima	Japan
	3	Matsuzaka	Japan
	3	Kiknadze	USSR
Open	1	Matsunaga	Japan
	2	Glahn	West Germany
	3	Shinomaki	Japan
	3	Herrmann	West Germany

Men's 6th World Judo Championships, Mexico City, Mexico, 1969

Category		Name	Country
u63k	1	Sonoda Y.	Japan
	2	Nomura	Japan
	3	Kim C.	South Korea
	3	Suslin	USSR
u78k	1	Minatoya	Japan
	2	Kono	Japan
	3	Rudmann	USSR
	3	Kim B.	South Korea
u80k	1	Sonoda	Japan
	2	Hirao	Japan
	3	Poklagen	Netherlands
	3	Ip	South Korea
u93k	1	Sasahara	Japan
	2	Herrmann	West Germany
	3	Kawabata	Japan
	3	Pokataer	USSR
o93k	1	Suma	Japan
	2	Glahn	West Germany
	3	Matsunaga	Japan
	3	Onashvilli	USSR
Open	1	Shinomaki	Japan
	2	Ruska	Netherlands
	3	Sato	Japan
	3	Eugster	Netherlands

Men's 7th World Judo Championships, Ludwigshafen, West Germany, 1971

Category		Name	Country
u63k	1	Kawaguchi	Japan
	2	Nomura	Japan
	3	Suslin	USSR
	3	Sam	South Korea
u70k	1	Tsuzawa	Japan
	2	Minatoya	Japan
	3	Hoetger	East Germany
	3	Zajkowski	Poland
u80k	1	Fuji	Japan
	2	Shigematsu	Japan
	3	Starbrook	Great Britain
	3	Auffray	France
u93k	1	Sasahara	Japan
	2	Sato	Japan
	3	Ishii	Brazil
	3	Howiller	East Germany

	1	Ruska	Netherlands
o93k	2	Glahn	West Germany
	3	Iwata	Japan
	3	Remfry	Great Britain
Open	1	Shinomaki	Japan
	2	Kusnetzov	USSR
	3	Sekine	Japan
	3	Glahn	West Germany

Men's 8th World Judo Championships, Lausanne, Switzerland, 1973

Category		Name	Country
u63k	1	Minami	Japan
	2	Kawaguchi	Japan
	3	Rodriquez	Cuba
	3	Pitschelauri	USSR
u70k	1	Nomura	Japan
	2	Hoetger	East Germany
	3	Yoshimura	Japan
	3	Novikov	USSR
u80k	1	Fuji	Japan
	2	Sonoda	Japan
	3	Reiter	Poland
	3	Look	East Germany
u93k	1	Sato	Japan
	2	Ueguchi	Japan
	3	Starbrook	Great Britain
	3	Lorenz	East Germany
o93k	1	Takagi	Japan
	2	Nizharadze	USSR
	3	Novikov	USSR
	3	Remfry	Great Britain
Open	1	Ninomiya	Japan
	2	Uemura	Japan
	3	Glahn	West Germany
	3	Zuckschwerdt	East Germany

Men's 9th World Judo Championships, Vienna, Austria, 1975

Category		Name	Country
u63k	1	Minami	Japan
	2	Kashiwazaki	Japan
	3	Reissman	East Germany
	3	Mariani	Italy

Category		Name	Country
u70k	1	Nevzorov	USSR
	2	Dvoinikov	USSR
	3	Kuramoto	Japan
	3	Akimoto	Japan
u80k	1	Fuji	Japan
	2	Hara	Japan
	3	Coche	France
	3	Adamczyk	Poland
u93k	1	Rouge	France
	2	Ishibashi	Japan
	3	Harshiladze	USSR
	3	Betanov	USSR
o93k	1	Endo	Japan
	2	Novikov	USSR
	3	Takaki	Japan
	3	Park	South Korea
Open	1	Uemura	Japan
	2	Ninomiya	Japan
	3	Chochoshvilli	USSR
	3	Lorenz	East Germany

Men's 10th World Judo Championships, Paris, France, 1979

Category		Name	Country
u60k	1	Rey	France
	2	Jong	South Korea
	3	Mariani	Italy
	3	Moriwaki	Japan
u65k	1	Soloduchin	USSR
	2	Delvingt	France
	3	Pawlowski	Poland
	3	Sahara	Japan
u71k	1	Katsuki	Japan
	2	Gamba	Italy
	3	Namgalauri	USSR
	3	Adams	Great Britain
u78k	1	Fuji	Japan
	2	Tchoullyan	France
	3	Heinke	East Germany
	3	Park	South Korea
u85k	1	Ultsch	East Germany
	2	Sanchis	France
	3	Takahashi	Japan
	3	Carmona	Brazil
u95k	1	Khouboulouri	USSR
	2	van de Walle	Belgium
	3	Numan	Netherlands
	3	Neureuther	West Germany

o95k	1	Yamashita	Japan
	2	Rouge	France
	3	Varga	Hungary
	3	Ki	South Korea
Open	1	Endo	Japan
	2	Kuznetsov	USSR
	3	Rouge	France
	3	Kovacevic	Yugoslavia

Men's 11th World Judo Championships, Maastricht, The Netherlands, 1981

Category		Name	Country
u60k	1	Moriwaki	Japan
	2	Petrikov	USSR
	3	Mariani	Italy
	3	Takahashi	Canada
u65k	1	Kashiwazaki	Japan
	2	Nicolae	Romania
	3	Ponomarev	USSR
	3	Hwang	South Korea
u71k	1	Ha	South Korea
	2	Dyot	France
	3	Vujevic	Yugoslavia
	3	Lehman	East Germany
u78k	1	Adams	Great Britain
	2	Kase	Japan
	3	Petrov	Bulgaria
	3	Doherty	Canada
u86k	1	Tchoullyan	France
	2	Nose	Japan
	3	Ultsch	East Germany
	3	Bodavelli	USSR
u95k	1	Khouboulouri	USSR
	2	van de Walle	Belgium
	3	Vachon	France
	3	Ha	South Korea
o95k	1	Yamashita	Japan
	2	Veritchev	USSR
	3	Kocman	USSR
	3	Salonen	Finland
Open	1	Yamashita	Japan
	2	Reszko	Poland
	3	van de Walle	Belgium
	3	Ozsvar	Hungary

Men's 12th World Judo Championships, Moscow, USSR, 1983

Category		Name	Country
u60k	1	Tletseri	USSR
	2	Bujko	Hungary
	3	Haraguchi	Japan
	3	Stollberg	East Germany
u65k	1	Soloduchin	USSR
	2	Matsuoka	Japan
	3	Pawlowski	Poland
	3	Rosati	Italy
u71k	1	Nakanishi	Japan
	2	Gamba	Italy
	3	Namgalauri	USSR
	3	Stranz	West Germany
u78k	1	Hikage	Japan
	2	Adams	Great Britain
	3	Khaberelli	USSR
	3	Fratica	Romania
u86k	1	Ultsch	East Germany
	2	Canu	France
	3	Berland	USA
	3	Nose	Japan
u95k	1	Preschel	East Germany
	2	Divisenko	USSR
	3	Neureuther	West Germany
	3	van de Walle	Belgium
o95k	1	Yamashita	Japan
	2	Wilhelm	Netherlands
	3	Stoehr	East Germany
	3	Cioc	Romania
Open	1	Saito	Japan
	2	Kocman	USSR
	3	Ozsvar	Hungary
	3	van de Walle	Belgium

Men's 13th World Judo Championships, Seoul, South Korea, 1985

Category		Name	Country
u60k	1	Hosokawa	Japan
	2	Jupke	West Germany
	3	Bujko	Hungary
	3	Tletseri	USSR
u65k	1	Sokolov	USSR
	2	Keun	South Korea
	3	Gawthorpe	Great Britain
	3	Matsuoka	Japan

	1	Keun	South Korea
u71k	2	Swain	USA
	3	Stranz	West Germany
	3	Blach	Poland
u78k	1	Hikage	Japan
	2	Ochnigen	East Germany
	3	Chestakov	USSR
	3	Adams	Great Britain
u86k	1	Seisenbacher	Austria
	2	Petrov	Bulgaria
	3	Canu	France
	3	Pesniak	USSR
u95k	1	Sugai	Japan
	2	Ha	South Korea
	3	Neureuther	West Germany
	3	van de Walle	Belgium
o95k	1	Cho	South Korea
	2	Saito	Japan
	3	Zaprianov	Bulgaria
	3	Veritchev	USSR
Open	1	Masaki	Japan
	2	Rashwan	Egypt
	3	Biktachev	USSR
	3	Wilhelm	Netherlands

Men's 14th World Judo Championships, Essen, West Germany, 1987

Category		Name	Country
u60k	1	Kim	South Korea
	2	Hosakawa	Japan
	3	Roux	France
	3	Asano	USA
u65k	1	Yamamoto	Japan
	2	Sokolov	USSR
	3	Bujko	Hungary
	3	Pawlowski	Poland
u71k	1	Swain	USA
	2	Alexandre	France
	3	Brown	Great Britain
	3	Koga	Japan
u78k	1	Okada	Japan
	2	Varaev	USSR
	3	Legien	Poland
	3	Lee	South Korea
u86k	1	Canu	France
	2	Pak	North Korea
	3	White	Great Britain
	3	Murata	Japan

u95k	1	Sugai	Japan
	2	Meyer	Netherlands
	3	Miguel	Brazil
	3	Ha	South Korea
o95k	1	Veritchev	USSR
	2	Rashwan	Egypt
	3	Xu	China
	3	Plate	West Germany
Open	1	Ogawa	Japan
	2	Gordon	Great Britain
	3	Stoehr	East Germany
	3	Castro	Cuba

Men's 15th World Judo Championships, Belgrade, Yugoslavia, 1989

Category		Name	Country
u60k	1	Totikachvilli	USSR
	2	Koshino	Japan
	3	Yoon	South Korea
	3	Dashgombyn	Mongolia
u65k	1	Becanovic	Yugoslavia
	2	Quelmalz	East Germany
	3	Kosmynin	USSR
	3	Carabetta	France
u71k	1	Koga	Japan
	2	Swain	USA
	3	Li	North Korea
	3	Tenadze	USSR
u78k	1	Ju	South Korea
	2	Mochida	Japan
	3	Varaev	USSR
	3	Legien	Poland
u86k	1	Canu	France
	2	Spykers	Netherlands
	3	Lobenstein	East Germany
	3	Freudenberg	West Germany
u95k	1	Kurtanidze	USSR
	2	Odvogin	Mongolia
	3	van de Walle	Belgium
	3	Meiling	West Germany
o95k	1	Ogawa	Japan
	2	Moreno	Cuba
	3	Veritchev	USSR
	3	Kubacki	Poland
Open	1	Ogawa	Japan
	2	Kibordalidze	USSR
	3	Kim	South Korea
	3	van der Groeben	West Germany

Men's 16th World Judo Championships, Barcelona, Spain, 1991

Category		Name	Country
u60k	1	Koshino	Japan
	2	Yoon	South Korea
	3	Gousseinov	* URS
	3	Pradayrol	France
u65k	1	Quellmalz	Germany
	2	Okuma	Japan
	3	Kosmynin	* URS
	3	Pedro	USA
u71k	1	Koga	Japan
	2	Ruiz	Spain
	3	Chung	North Korea
	3	Dguebouadze	* URS
u78k	1	Lascau	Germany
	2	Laats	Belgium
	3	Varaev	* URS
	3	Yoshida	Japan
u86k	1	Okada	Japan
	2	Wanag	USA
	3	Legien	Poland
	3	Vismara	Italy
u95k	1	Traineau	France
	2	Nastula	Poland
	3	Meiling	Germany
	3	Sosna	Czechoslovakia
o95k	1	Kosorotov	* URS
	2	Moreno	Cuba
	3	Ogawa	Japan
	3	Kim	North Korea
Open	1	Ogawa	Japan
	2	Khakhaleichvili	* URS
	3	Mathonnet	France
	3	Csosz	Hungary

* Union of Russian States

Men's 17th World Judo Championships, Hamilton, Canada, 1993

Category		Name	Country
u60k	1	Sonoda	Japan
	2	Gusseinov	Azerbaijan
	3	Vazagachvili	Georgia
	3	Trautmann	Germany
u65k	1	Nakamura	Japan
	2	Born	Switzerland
	3	Kosmiynin	Russia
	3	Quellmalz	Germany
u71k	1	Chung	North Korea
	2	Hajtos	Hungary
	3	Hideshima	Japan
	3	Sampaio-Cardoso	Brazil
u78k	1	Ki-Young	South Korea
	2	Yoshida	Japan
	3	Yandzi	France
	3	Morris	USA
u86k	1	Nakamura	Japan
	2	Gill	Canada
	3	Villar-Beltran	Spain
	3	Croitoru	Romania
u95k	1	Kovacs	Hungary
	2	Miguel	Brazil
	3	Traineau	France
	3	Meilling	Germany
o95k	1	Douillet	France
	2	Khakhaleishvili	Georgia
	3	Kosorotov	Russia
	3	Möller	Germany
Open	1	Kubacki	Poland
	2	Stohr	Germany
	3	Ogawa	Japan
	3	Khakhaleishvili	Georgia

Men's 18th World Judo Championships, Tokyo, Japan, 1995

Category		Name	Country
u60k	1	Ojeguine	Russia
	2	Vazagachvili	Georgia
	3	Bagirov	Belgium
	3	Sonoda	Japan
u65k	1	Quellmalz	Germany
	2	Nakamura	Japan
	3	Kim	South Korea
	3	Demirel	Turkey
u71k	1	Hideshima	Japan
	2	Kwak	South Korea
	3	Brambilla	Italy
	3	Pedro	USA
u78k	1	Koga	Japan
	2	Smadga	Israel
	3	Reiter	Austria
	3	Bouras	France
u86k	1	Jeon	South Korea
	2	Yoshida	Japan
	3	Maltsev	Russia
	3	Gill	Canada
u95k	1	Nastula	Poland
	2	Sergueev	Russia
	3	Traineau	France
	3	Okaizuma	Japan
o95k	1	Douillet	France
	2	Möller	Germany
	3	Khakhaleishvili	Georgia
	3	Ogawa	Japan
Open	1	Douillet	France
	2	Kosorotov	Russia
	3	Tataroglu	Turkey
	3	Shinohara	Japan

WORLD CHAMPIONSHIPS

Women's 1st World Judo Championships, New York, United States, 1980

Category		Name	Country
u48k	1	Bridge	Great Britain
	2	De Novellis	Italy
	3	Colignon	France
	3	Lewis	USA
u52k	1	Hrovat	Austria
	2	Yamaguchi	Japan
	3	McCarthy	Great Britain
	3	Doger	France
u56k	1	Winklbauer	Austria
	2	Panza	France
	3	Doyle	Great Britain
	3	Meulemans	Belgium
u61k	1	Staps	Netherlands
	2	Di Toma	Italy
	3	Rottier	France
	3	Berg	West Germany
u66k	1	Simon	Austria
	2	Netherwood	Great Britain
	3	Penick	USA
	3	Peirre	France
u72k	1	Triadou	France
	2	Classen	West Germany
	3	Van Meggelen	Netherlands
	3	Malley	Great Britain
o72k	1	De Cal	Italy
	2	Fouillet	France
	3	Keiburg	West Germany
	3	Berghmans	Belgium
Open	1	Berghmans	Belgium
	2	Fouillet	France
	3	Classen	West Germany
	3	Fest	USA

Women's 2nd World Judo Championships, Paris, France, 1982

Category		Name	Country
u48k	1	Briggs	Great Britain
	2	Colignon	France
	3	Nakahara	Japan
	3	Bink	Netherlands
u52k	1	Doyle	Great Britain
	2	Yamaguchi	Japan
	3	Doger	France
	3	Boyd	Australia
u56k	1	Rodriquez	France
	2	Williams	Australia
	3	Hernandez	Venezuela
	3	Bell	Great Britain
u61k	1	Rottier	France
	2	Solheim	Norway
	3	Peeters	Belgium
	3	Ritchel	West Germany
u66k	1	Deydier	France
	2	Kruger	West Germany
	3	Andersen	Norway
	3	Staps	Netherlands
u72k	1	Classen	West Germany
	2	Berghmans	Belgium
	3	Triadou	France
	3	Posch	Austria
o72k	1	Lupino	France
	2	Castro	USA
	3	Van Unen	Netherlands
	3	Motta	Italy
Open	1	Berghmans	Belgium
	2	Tateishi	Japan
	3	Triadou	France
	3	Sigmund	West Germany

Women's 3rd World Judo Championships, Vienna, Austria, 1984

Category		Name	Country
u48k	1	Briggs	Great Britain
	2	Colignon	France
	3	Reardon	Australia
	3	Anaya	USA
u52k	1	Yamaguchi	Japan
	2	Hrovat	Austria
	3	Boyd	Australia
	3	Majdan	Poland
u56k	1	Burns	USA
	2	Williams	Australia
	3	Winklbauer	Austria
	3	Arnaud	France
u61k	1	Hernandez	Venezuela
	2	Han	Netherlands
	3	Rottier	France
	3	Hashinoe	Japan
u66k	1	Deydier	France
	2	De Kok	Netherlands
	3	Netherwood	Great Britain
	3	Kandori	Japan
u72k	1	Berghmans	Belgium
	2	Classen	West Germany
	3	Staps	Netherlands
	3	Vigneron	France
o72k	1	Motta	Italy
	2	Gao	China
	3	Castro	USA
	3	Van Unen	Netherlands
Open	1	Berghmans	Belgium
	2	Van Unen	Netherlands
	3	Lupino	France
	3	Gao	China

Womens 4th World Judo Championships, Maastricht, The Netherlands, 1986

Category		Name	Country
u48k	1	Briggs	Great Britain
	2	Ezaki	Japan
	3	Boffin	France
	3	Zhangyun	China
u52k	1	Brun	France
	2	Yamaguchi	Japan
	3	Sook Ok	South Korea
	3	Rendle	Great Britain

	1	Hughes	Great Britain
u56k	2	Gontowicz	Poland
	3	Rodriguez	France
	3	Gross	Netherlands
u61k	1	Bell	Great Britain
	2	Geraud	France
	3	Guy	New Zealand
	3	Fujimoto	Japan
u66k	1	Deydier	France
	2	Karlsson	Sweden
	3	Staps	Netherlands
	3	Schreiber	West Germany
u72k	1	De Kok	Netherlands
	2	Berghmans	Belgium
	3	Lin	China
	3	Classens	West Germany
o72k	1	Gao	China
	2	Van Unen	Netherlands
	3	Santini	Puerto Rico
	3	Paque	France
Open	1	Berghmans	Belgium
	2	Ling Li	China
	3	Meignan	France
	3	Kutz	West Germany

Women's 5th World Judo Championships, Essen, West Germany, 1987

Category		Name	Country
u48k	1	Li	China
	2	Esaki	Japan
	3	Chou	Taiwan
	3	Gal	Netherlands
u52k	1	Rendle	Great Britain
	2	Yamaguchi	Japan
	3	Giungi	Italy
	3	Brun	France
u56k	1	Arnaud	France
	2	Williams	Australia
	3	Hughes	Great Britain
	3	Philips	West Germany
u61k	1	Bell	Great Britain
	2	Roethke	USA
	3	Mochida	Japan
	3	Olechinowicz	Poland
u66k	1	Schreiber	West Germany
	2	Deydier	France
	3	Hartl	Austria
	3	Sasaki	Japan

u72k			
	1	De Kok	Netherlands
	2	Berghmans	Belgium
	3	Tanabe	Japan
	3	Classen	West Germany

o72k			
	1	Gao	China
	2	Sigmund	West Germany
	3	Seriese	Netherlands
	3	Castro-Gomez	USA

Open			
	1	Gao	China
	2	Berghmans	Belgium
	3	Paque	France
	3	Kutz	West Germany

Women's 6th World Judo Championships, Belgrade, Yugoslavia, 1989

Category		Name	Country
u48k	1	Briggs	Great Britain
	2	Esaki	Japan
	3	Gal	Netherlands
	3	Nowak	France
u52k	1	Rendle	Great Britain
	2	Giungi	Italy
	3	Perez	Cuba
	3	Cho	South Korea
u56k	1	Arnaud	France
	2	Hughes	Great Britain
	3	Blasco	Spain
	3	Yong	South Korea
u61k	1	Fleury	France
	2	Petrova	USSR
	3	Ritschel	West Germany
	3	Kobayashi	Japan
u66k	1	Pierantozzi	Italy
	2	Sasaki	Japan
	3	Lecat	France
	3	Reve	Cuba
u72k	1	Berghmans	Belgium
	2	Tanabe	Japan
	3	Batailler	France
	3	Wu	China
o72k	1	Gao	China
	2	Sigmund	West Germany
	3	Lupino	France
	3	Maksymow	Poland
Open	1	Rodriguez	Cuba
	2	Lee	Great Britain
	3	Tanabe	Japan
	3	Zhang	China

Women's 7th World Judo Championships, Barcelona, Spain, 1991

Category		Name	Country
u48k	1	Nowak	France
	2	Briggs	Great Britain
	3	Tamura	Japan
	3	Verdecia	Cuba
u52k	1	Giungi	Italy
	2	Rendle	Great Britain
	3	Perez	Cuba
	3	Ueda	Japan
u56k	1	Blasco	Spain
	2	Flagothier	Belgium
	3	Fairbrother	Great Britain
	3	Li	China
u61k	1	Eickoff	Germany
	2	Bell	Great Britain
	3	Fleury	France
	3	Arad	Israel
u66k	1	Pierantozzi	Italy
	2	Reve	Cuba
	3	Fujimoto	Japan
	3	Howey	Great Britain
u72k	1	Kim	South Korea
	2	Tanabe	Japan
	3	van Dorssen	Netherlands
	3	Meignan	France
o72k	1	Moon	South Korea
	2	Zhang	China
	3	Maksymow	Poland
	3	van der Lee	Netherlands
Open	1	Zhuang	China
	2	Rodriguez	Cuba
	3	Weber	Germany
	3	Lupino	France

Women's 8th World Judo Championships, Hamilton, Canada, 1993

Category		Name	Country
u48k	1	Tamura	Japan
	2	Li	China
	3	Heron	Great Britain
	3	Tortora	Italy
u52k	1	Verdecia-Rodriquez	Cuba
	2	Munoz	Spain
	3	Nowak	France
	3	Suzuki	Japan
u56k	1	Fairbrother	Great Britain
	2	Tateno	Japan
	3	Gal	Netherlands
	3	Gonzalez-Morales	Cuba
u61k	1	Vandecaveye	Belgium
	2	Arad	Israel
	3	Bell	Great Britain
	3	Beltran-Zulueta	Cuba
u66k	1	Cho	South Korea
	2	Ogasawara	USA
	3	Reve-Jimenez	Cuba
	3	Zhang	China
u72k	1	Leng	China
	2	Howey	Great Britain
	3	Kazounina	Russia
	3	Kim	South Korea
o72k	1	Hagn	Germany
	2	Anno	Japan
	3	van der Lee	Netherlands
	3	Gondarenko	Russia
Open	1	Maksymow	Poland
	2	Seriese	Netherlands
	3	Zhang	China
	3	Moon	South Korea

Women's 9th World Judo Championships, Tokyo, Japan, 1995

Category		Name	Country
u48k	1	Tamura	Japan
	2	Li	China
	3	Savon-Carmenaty	Cuba
	3	Roszowska	Poland
u52k	1	Restoux	France
	2	Mariani-Ambruesa	Argentina
	3	Rendle	Great Britain
	3	Verdecia-Rodriguez	Cuba
u56k	1	Gonzalez-Morales	Cuba
	2	Jung	South Korea
	3	Zangrando	Brazil
	3	Cavalleri	Portugal
u61k	1	Jung	South Korea
	2	Gal	Netherlands
	3	Vandecaveye	Belgium
	3	Fleury-Vachon	France
u66k	1	Cho	South Korea
	2	Reve-Jimenez	Cuba
	3	Ogasawara	USA
	3	Szczepanska	Poland
u72k	1	Luna	Cuba
	2	Werbrouck	Belgium
	3	Beliaeva	Ukraine
	3	Tanabe	Japan
o72k	1	Seriese	Netherlands
	2	Zhang	China
	3	Beltran-Guisado	Cuba
	3	Shan	South Korea
Open	1	van der Lee	Netherlands
	2	Sun	China
	3	Lee	South Korea
	3	Rodriquez-Villanueva	Cuba

OLYMPIC GAMES

1964 Tokyo Olympic Games

Category		Name	Country
u68k	1	Nakatani	Japan
	2	Haenni	Switzerland
	3	Stepanov	USSR
	3	Bogolubov	USSR
u80k	1	Okano	Japan
	2	Hofmann	West Germany
	3	Kim	South Korea
	3	Bregman	USA
o80k	1	Inokuma	Japan
	2	Rogers	Canada
	3	Kiknadze	USSR
	3	Chikviladze	USSR
Open	1	Geesink	Netherlands
	2	Kaminaga	Japan
	3	Glahn	West Germany
	3	Boronovskis	Austria

1972 Munich Olympic Games

Category		Name	Country
u63k	1	Kawaguchi	Japan
	2	Buidaa	Mongolia
	3	Mounier	France
	3	Kim	South Korea
u70k	1	Nomura	Japan
	2	Zajkowski	Poland
	3	Novikov	USSR
	3	Hoetger	East Germany
u80k	1	Sekine	Japan
	2	Oh	South Korea
	3	Coche	France
	3	Jacks	Great Britain
u93k	1	Chochoshvili	USSR
	2	Starbrook	Great Britain
	3	Barth	West Germany
	3	Ishii	Brazil
o93k	1	Ruska	Netherlands
	2	Glahn	West Germany
	3	Nishimura	Japan
	3	Onashvilli	USSR
Open	1	Ruska	Netherlands
	2	Kusnezov	USSR
	3	Brondani	France
	3	Parisi	France

	1	Parisi	France
o95k	2	Zaprianov	Bulgaria
	3	Kocman	USSR
	3	Kovacevic	Yugoslavia
Open	1	Lorenz	East Germany
	2	Parisi	France
	3	Mapp	Great Britain
	3	Ozsvar	Hungary

1976 Montreal Olympic Games

Category		Name	Country
u63k	1	Rodriguez	Cuba
	2	Chang	South Korea
	3	Tunosil	Hungary
	3	Mariani	Italy
u70k	1	Nevzorov	USSR
	2	Kuramoto	Japan
	3	Vial	France
	3	Talaj	Poland
u80k	1	Sonoda	Japan
	2	Dvoinikov	USSR
	3	Obadov	Yugoslavia
	3	Park	South Korea
u93k	1	Ninomiya	Japan
	2	Harshiladze	USSR
	3	Starbrook	Great Britain
	3	Roethlisberger	Switzerland
o93k	1	Novikov	USSR
	2	Neureuther	West Germany
	3	Coage	USA
	3	Endo	Japan
Open	1	Uemura	Japan
	2	Remfry	Great Britain
	3	Chochoshvili	USSR
	3	Cho	South Korea

1980 Moscow Olympic Games

Category		Name	Country
u60k	1	Rey	France
	2	Rodriguez	Cuba
	3	Emizh	USSR
	3	Kincses	Hungary
u65k	1	Solduchin	USSR
	2	Damden	Mongolia
	3	Nedkov	Bulgaria
	3	Pawlowski	Poland
u71k	1	Gamba	Italy
	2	Adams	Great Britain
	3	Dawaadalia	Mongolia
	3	Lehman	East Germany
u78k	1	Kharbarelli	USSR
	2	Ferrer	Cuba
	3	Heinke	East Germany
	3	Tchoullyan	France
u86k	1	Roethlisberger	Switzerland
	2	Azcuy	Cuba
	3	Yaskevitch	USSR
	3	Ultsch	East Germany
u95k	1	van de Walle	Belgium
	2	Khouboulouri	USSR
	3	Lorenz	East Germany
	3	Numan	Netherlands
o95k	1	Parisi	France
	2	Zaprianov	Bulgaria
	3	Kockman	USSR
	3	Kovacevic	Yugoslavia
Open	1	Lorenz	West Germany
	2	Parisi	France
	3	Mapp	Great Britain
	3	Ozsvar	Hungary

1984 Los Angeles Olympic Games

Category		Name	Country
u60k	1	Hosakawa	Japan
	2	Kim	South Korea
	3	Little	USA
	3	Eckersley	Great Britain
u65k	1	Matsuoka	Japan
	2	Hwang	South Korea
	3	Alexandre	France
	3	Reiter	Austria

	1	Ahn	South Korea
u71k	2	Gamba	Italy
	3	Brown	Great Britain
	3	Onmura	Brazil
u78k	1	Wienecke	West Germany
	2	Adams	Great Britain
	3	Fratica	Romania
	3	Nowak	France
u86k	1	Seisenbacher	Austria
	2	Berland	USA
	3	Carmona	Brazil
	3	Nose	Japan
u95k	1	Ha	South Korea
	2	Vieira	Brazil
	3	Friedriksson	Iceland
	3	Neureuther	West Germany
o95k	1	Saito	Japan
	2	Parisi	France
	3	Cho	South Korea
	3	Berger	Canada
Open	1	Yamashita	Japan
	2	Rashwan	Egypt
	3	Cioc	Romania
	3	Schnabel	West Germany

1988 Seoul Olympic Games, South Korea

Category		Name	Country
u60k	1	Kim	South Korea
	2	Asano	USA
	3	Hosakawa	Japan
	3	Totikachvilli	USSR
u65k	1	Lee	South Korea
	2	Pawlowski	Poland
	3	Carabetta	France
	3	Yamamoto	Japan
u71k	1	Alexandre	France
	2	Loll	East Germany
	3	Tenadze	USSR
	3	Swain	USA
u78k	1	Legien	Poland
	2	Wienecke	West Germany
	3	Brechot	East Germany
	3	Varaev	USSR
u86k	1	Seisenbacher	Austria
	2	Chestakov	USSR
	3	Spijkers	Netherlands
	3	Osako	Japan

		Name	Country
u95k	1	Miguel	Brazil
	2	Meiling	West Germany
	3	van de Valle	Belgium
	3	Stewart	East Germany
o95k	1	Saito	Japan
	2	Stoehr	East Germany
	3	Veritchev	USSR
	3	Cho	South Korea

1992 Barcelona Olympic Games, Spain

Category		Name	Country
u60k	1	Gousscinov	* EUN
	2	Yoon	South Korea
	3	Koshino	Japan
	3	Trautmann	Germany
u65k	1	Sampaio	Brazil
	2	Csak	Hungary
	3	Quellmalz	Germany
	3	Hernandez	Cuba
u71k	1	Koga	Japan
	2	Hajtos	Hungary
	3	Chung	North Korea
	3	Smadga	Israel
u78k	1	Yoshida	Japan
	2	Morris	USA
	3	Damaisin	France
	3	Kim	South Korea
u86k	1	Legien	Poland
	2	Tayot	France
	3	Okada	Japan
	3	Gill	Canada
u95k	1	Kovacs	Hungary
	2	Stevens	Great Britain
	3	Maijerrs	Netherlands
	3	Sergeev	* EUN
o95k	1	Khakhaleichvili	* EUN
	2	Ogawa	Japan
	3	Douillet	Hungary
	3	Csosz	Belgium

* Unified Team of the former Soviet Union

1996 Atlanta Olympic Games

Category		Name	Country
u60k	1	Nomura	Japan
	2	Giovinazzo	Italy
	3	Narmanbakh	Mongolia
	3	Trautmann	Germany
u65k	1	Quellmalz	Germany
	2	Nakamura	Japan
	3	Hernandez	Cuba
	3	Guimares	Brazil
u71k	1	Hideshima	Japan
	2	Kwak	South Korea
	3	Gagliano	France
	3	Pedro	USA
u78k	1	Bouras	France
	2	Koga	Japan
	3	Chul	Korea
	3	Liparteliani	Georgia
u86k	1	Jeon	South Korea
	2	Bagdasarov	Uzbekistan
	3	Huizinga	Netherlands
	3	Spitka	Germany
u95k	1	Nastula	Poland
	2	Kim	South Korea
	3	Traineau	France
	3	Miguel	Brazil
o95k	1	Douillet	France
	2	Perez	Spain
	3	Möller	Germany
	3	van Barneveldt	Belgium

Women's Demonstration Event, Seoul, South Korea, 1988

Category		Name	Country
u48k	1	Li	China
	2	Esaki	Japan
	3	Reardon	Australia
	3	Cho	South Korea
u52k	1	Rendle	Great Britain
	2	Brun	France
	3	Giungi	Italy
	3	Yamaguchi	Japan
u55k	1	Williams	Australia
	2	Liu	China
	3	Arnaud	France
	3	Phillips	West Germany
u61k	1	Bell	Great Britain
	2	Roethke	USA
	3	Mochida	Japan
	3	Olechnowicz	Poland
u65k	1	Sasaki	Japan
	2	Deydier	France
	3	Hartl	Austria
	3	Park	South Korea
u72k	1	Bergmahns	Belgium
	2	Bae	South Korea
	3	Classens	West Germany
	3	Tanabe	Japan
o72k	1	Seriese	Netherlands
	2	Gao	China
	3	Sigmund	West Germany
	3	Gomez	USA

Women's Judo Championships, 1992 Barcelona Olympic Games

Category		Name	Country
u48k	1	Nowak	France
	2	Tamura	Japan
	3	Senyurt	Turkey
	3	Savon	Cuba
u52k	1	Muñoz	Spain
	2	Mizoguchi	Japan
	3	Li	China
	3	Rendle	Great Britain
u56k	1	Blasco	Spain
	2	Fairbrother	Great Britain
	3	Tateno	Japan
	3	Gonzalez	Cuba

Category		Name	Country
u61k	1	Fleury	France
	2	Arad	Israel
	3	Zhang	China
	3	Petrova	* EUN
u66k	1	Reve	Cuba
	2	Pierantozzi	Italy
	3	Rakels	Belgium
	3	Howey	Great Britain
u72k	1	Kim	South Korea
	2	Tanabe	Japan
	3	Meignan	France
	3	de Kok	Netherlands
o72k	1	Zhuang	China
	2	Rodriquez	Cuba
	3	Sakaue	Japan
	3	Lupino	France

*Unified Team of the former Soviet Union

Women's Judo Championships, 1996 Atlanta Olympic Games

Category		Name	Country
u48k	1	Sun	North Korea
	2	Tamura	Japan
	3	Savon-Carmenaty	Cuba
	3	Soler	Spain
u52k	1	Restoux	France
	2	Hee	South Korea
	3	Verdecia-Rodriguez	Cuba
	3	Sugawara	Japan
u56k	1	Gonzalez-Morales	Cuba
	2	Jung	South Korea
	3	Fernandez	Spain
	3	Lomba	Belgium
u61k	1	Emato	Japan
	2	Vandekeveye	Belgium
	3	Jung	South Korea
	3	Gal	Netherlands
u66k	1	Cho	South Korea
	2	Szczepanska	Poland
	3	Zwiers	Belgium
	3	Xiando	China
u72k	1	Werbrouck	Belgium
	2	Tanabe	Japan
	3	Scapin	Italy
	3	Luna	Cuba
o72k	1	Sun	China
	2	Rodriguez	Cuba
	3	Cicot	France
	3	Hagen	Germany

Glossary

Ago-oshi   Pushing; chin.
Aiki   A form of self-defence, based on special principles (lit. harmony of spirit).
Aikido   The 'way' of Aiki.
Aite   Opponent, partner.
Arashi   Storm (e.g. *Yama-arashi*; mountain storm).
Ashiwaza   Leg or foot technique.
Atama   Head.
Ate   Strike, hit, punch or kick.
Atemiwaza   Striking techniques using hand, elbow, knee, foot etc.
Bo-jutsu   Stick or staff fighting.
Bu   Martial or military.
Chui   Penalty (equivalent to five points).
Dan   Step. A black-belt holder.
De (v. deru)   To come out, to advance (e.g. *De-ashi-barai*).
Do   (a) Way, path, etc. This word was frequently used in Chinese and Japanese philosophy in the sense of the way of doing an act in the moral and ethical sphere as well as the physical. Kano 'borrowed' it from these sources. (b) Trunk of the body.
Dojo   Training hall or room in which judo is practised.
Eri   Collar, lapel.
Eri-jime   Strangulation by use of collar.
Gake (v. kakeru)   To hang, hook, block.
Garami (v. garamu)   To entangle, wrap, bend.
Gari   To reap, as with a scythe.
Gasshuku   Judo students lodging together for training.
Gokyo   The forty (original) throws in judo.
Gono-sen-no-kata   Forms of counter technique.
Go-shin-jutsu   The art of self-protection (in all its forms).

Gyaku   Reverse, upside-down.
Ha   Wing.
Hadaka   Naked.
Hajime   Start, referee's call to commence a contest.
Hane   Spring (e.g. *Hane-goshi*; spring hip).
Hansoku-make   Loss by disqualification (penalty equivalent to ten points).
Hantei   Judgement, the referee's call at the end of a drawn contest, requesting the corner judges to indicate who, in their opinion, was the better of the two contestants.
Hara   Stomach.
Harai, barai (v. harau)   To clear away, sweep.
Harai-goshi   Sweeping loin throw.
Harai-tsuri-komi-ashi   Sweeping drawing ankle.
Hidari   Left side.
Hiji   Elbow (e.g. *Hiji-ate*; to hit with the elbow).
Hikki (v. hikku)   To pull.
Hikki-waki   A draw in contest.
Hiza   Knee.
Hiza-guruma   Knee wheel.
Hon   (a) Basic. (b) Number suffix for counting long cylindrical objects, therefore *Ippon-seoi-nage*; one-arm shoulder throw.
Ippon   One point (score value of ten points).
Itsutsu-no-kata   Forms of five (the five elements/principles).
Jigotai   Defensive posture.
Jikan   Time (time out).
Jita-kyoei   The principle that individual advancement benefits society as a whole.
Joseki   The place in a dojo or hall where the seniors or VIPs sit.
Ju   (a) Soft gentle. This word is taken from Taoist philosophy and embodies the opposite

of hard, extreme, unreasonable. Hence the use of 'ju' in judo does not imply soft (as a synonym of easy), but rather reasonable, efficient. Physical action in judo is not meant to be easy (weak) so much as economic. By using the body to its best advantage and exploiting the weaknesses of the opponent, maximum effect can be obtained with maximum efficiency. (b) Ten.

Ju jitsu, ju jutsu, jui jitsu   A name covering many forms of close combat in Japan.

Judo   An Olympic sport, combat, art, derived from the ancient arts of ju jitsu by the founder Jigoro Kano.

Judogi   The clothes worn when practising or competing at judo, comprising jacket, trousers and belt.

Judoka   A high-grade judo player, but used in the West as a convenient word to describe anybody who practises judo.

Juji-jime   Normal cross strangle.

Ju-no-kata   The forms of 'gentleness'.

Kaeshi, gaeshi   In judo this means 'counter' (e.g. *Osoto-gaeshi*; major outer counter).

Kaeshiwaza   Technique of counter throw.

Kai, kwai   Society, club.

Kake   The point of the throw, the point of maximum power.

Kame   (a) Upper, top. (b) Paper. (c) God(s).

Kani-basami   'Scissors' throw.

Kansetsu   A joint (of the body).

Kansetsuwaza   A joint technique. (In judo only elbow locks are permitted, but this term can be used to describe a lock on any joint.).

Kao   Face.

Karate   Literally 'empty-handed'; a system of fighting without weapons, striking the hands, feet, elbows, etc.

Kata   (a) Form. A training method used in judo and most martial arts, a drill. (b) One of a pair. (c) Shoulder (e.g. *Kata-guruma*; shoulder wheel).

Kata-guruma   Shoulder wheel.

Kata-ha-jime   Shoulder wing choke-lock.

Kata-juji-jime   Half-cross strangle.

Katame, gatame (v. katemeru)   To harden.

Katamewaza   Groundwork technique.

Katsu, kappo   Methods of resuscitation.

Keiko   Practice.

Keikoku   Severe penalty (equivalent to seven points).

Kempo   A method of fighting founded in Shorinji similar to ju jitsu.

Ken   Sword.

Kendo   The 'way' of the sword (Japanese two-handed fencing).

Kesa   A Buddhist monk's surplice, worn diagonally across the body, thus the technique known as *Kesa-gatame*, freely translated into English as scarf hold.

Ki   Psychic energy said to be centred in the *saikatanden*.

Kiai   A shout used to harden the body and strengthen the will when maximum effort is required.

Kime (v. kakeru)   To decide.

Kime-no-kata   Forms of decision, which are the kata of self-protection.

Kiri (v. kiru)   To cut, as with a knife.

Ko   (a) Small, minor (e.g. *Kouchi-gari*; minor inner reap). (b) Old, ancient.

Kodokan   The headquarters of judo in Japan (Tokyo); the founder's dojo.

Koka   A score, almost a yuko (score value of three points).

Koshi, goshi   Hips (e.g. koshiwaza; hip techniques).

Koshi-guruma   Hip wheel.

Kosoto-gake   Minor outside hook.

Kosoto-gari   Minor outside reap.

Kouchi-gari   Minor inner reap.

Kubi   Neck.

Kumikata   The method of grappling of two contestants.

Kuruka, guruma   (a) Wheel (e.g. *Oguruma*; major wheel). (b) Vehicle.

Kuzure (v. kuzureru)   To crumble, collapse, break down. Thus a free translation of *Kuzure-kesa-gatame* would be broken scarf hold. A hold that is not quite the basic or pure form (hon).

Kuzure-kame-shiho-gatame   Broken upper four quarters.

Kuzushi   The balance broken.

Kyu   A judo 'student' grade.

Ma   Direct, exact, absolutely (e.g. Masute-miwaza; direct sacrifice throw to the rear).

Machi-dojo   Street dojo, small local dojo.

Mae   Front.

Makikomi   Winding, to wrap or roll up, to throw by rolling oneself so that the opponent is 'locked on' to one's body.

Ma-sutemi-waza   Technique whereby the performer (tori) falls straight on to his back to throw.

Mata   The thigh.

Matte   Refereeing word meaning 'wait'.

Migi   Right side.

Mizu   Water.

Mon   Gate, junior grade.

Morote   Both hands (e.g. *Morote-seoi-nage*; two-handed shoulder throw).

Morote-gari   Two-handed throw by clasping opponent's legs.

Mune   Chest (e.g. *Mune-gatame*; chest hold).

Nage (v. nageru)   To throw (e.g. nagewaza; throwing techniques).

Nage-no-kata   The forms of throwing, fifteen selected throws executed both left and right to train the participants in body control and appreciation of judo technique.

Name   Wave (of water).

Nami   In a line, in a row.

Ne (v. neru)   To lie down.

Newaza   Technique carried out in a lying-down position.

No   Belonging to. A link word as in *Nage-no-kata*.

O   Big, large, major (e.g. Ouchi-gari; major inner reaping).

Obi   Belt.

Ogoshi   Major hip technique.

Oguruma   Major wheel.

Okuri (v. okuru)   To send forward.

Okuri-ashi-barai   Sweeping ankle throw.

Okuri-eri-jime   Sliding collar strangle.

Osaekomi   Holding (e.g. osaekomiwaza; holding techniques); referee's call signalling that a hold is effective.

Oshi (v. osu)   To push.

Osoto-gari   Major outer reaping.

Osoto-otoshi   Major outer drop.

Otoshi (v. otosu)   To drop.

Ouchi-gari   Major inner reaping.

Ouchimata   Major or great inner thigh.

Randori   Free practice.

Rei   Bow.

Renraku   Connection, communication, contact.

Renrakuwaza   Combination technique.

Renshu   Free practice or exercise.

Renzokuwaza   Comprehensive name for techniques linked up in any way.

Ryote   Two hands.

Ryu   Method or style. Attached to most of the names of the old ju jitsu systems (e.g. Kito Ryu).

Sasae   To support, prop (e.g. *Sasae-tsuri-komi-ashi*; propping drawing ankle).

Sei-ryoku-senyo   The principle of maximum efficiency in the use of mind and body.

Sensei   Teacher, Master (or person of high standing).

Senshu   A competitor, champion.

Seoi (v. seou)   To carry on the back (translated into English, *Seoi-nage* is more commonly known as 'shoulder throw').

Seoi-otoshi   Shoulder drop.

Shiai   Contest.

Shido   Note (penalty equivalent to three points).

Shihan   Master, past-master.

Shiho   Four quarters, four directions.

Shiki   Style, ceremony.

Shime, jime (v. shimeru)   To tighten, strangle.

Shimewaza   Technique of strangling.

Shizentai   Natural (upright) posture.

Sode   Sleeve.

Sode-tsuri-komi-goshi   Sleeve resisting hip throw.

Sogo-gachi   Compound win by ippon made up of a score of waza-ari added to the benefit of a keikoku penalty.

Sono-mama   Freeze, do not move (referee's instruction to the two combatants in a contest when he requires them to stay absolutely still).

189

Sore-made   That is all, finish (referee's command terminating the contest).
Soto   Outside, outer (e.g. *Osoto-gari*; major outer reap).
Sukui (v. sukuu)   To scoop up.
Sumi   Corner.
Sutemi (v. suteru)   To throw away.
Sutemiwaza   Technique whereby the attacker sacrifices his own posture.
Tachi (v. tatsu)   To stand.
Tachi-rei   Standing bow.
Tachiwaza   Technique performed in the standing position.
Tai   Body.
Tai-sabaki   Body movement.
Tani   Valley (e.g. *Tani-otoshi*; valley drop).
Tatami   Rice straw mats used in dojos and Japanese houses.
Tate   Vertical.
Te   Hand (e.g. tewaza; hand techniques).
Tekubi   Wrist.
Toketa   Hold broken. A command given by the referee to indicate to the timekeeper that the 'count must stop' when a contestant has effectively broken the hold by which he was being secured.
Tokui   Favourite, special (e.g. tokui waza; favourite technique).
Tomoe   Turning over, twisting over, whirling over. It is difficult to find the exact translation in English, but *Tomoe-nage* freely translated is commonly known in English as stomach throw.
Tori (v. toru)   (a) The name used often in technical explanation for the person who applies the technique. (b) To grasp, to hold in the hands.
Tsugi-ashi   A manner of walking in which one foot leads at each step and the other never passes it.
Tsukiwaza   Poke, stab, thrust or punch technique.
Tsukuri (v. tsukuru)   The action of breaking the opponent's balance.

Tsuri   To 'fish' up (e.g. *Tsuri-komi*; lift up and pull forward).
Tsuri-komi-goshi   Resisting hip throw.
Uchikomi (v. utsukomu)   To beat against, go in. A repetitive exercise where the throwing technique is taken to the point of kake.
Uchimata   Inner thigh.
Ude   Arm.
Ude-garami   Arm entanglement.
Ue   Above, on top of.
Uke (v. ukeru)   To receive. The name often used in technical explanations for the person on whom the technique is applied.
Ukemi   The 'breakfall'.
Uki (v. uku)   To float, buoyant.
Uki-goshi   Floating hip.
Ura   Back, rear (e.g. *Uranage*; rear throw).
Ushiro   Behind, back of (e.g. *Ushiro-jime*; any strangle from behind).
Utsuri (v. utsuru)   To change, to move (e.g. *Utsuri-goshi*; changing hip).
Wakare (v. wakareru)   To divide separate (e.g. *Yoko-wakare*; side separation).
Waki   Armpit.
Waza   Technique.
Waza-ari   A score, almost an ippon (score value of seven points).
Waza-ari awesete ippon   Ippon achieved by having scored two waza-ari.
Yama   Mountain.
Yoko   Side (e.g. *Yoko-shiho-gatame*; side four quarters).
Yoko-sutemiwaza   Side sacrifice throw.
Yoshi   Let's go, let's get on with it. Referee's instruction used after sono-mama to resume the contest.
Yuko   A score, almost waza-ari (score value of five points).
Yusei-gachi   A win by superiority.
Za-rei   Formal kneeling bow or salutation.
Za-zen   Kneeling motionless in concentrated thought, meditation.
Zori   Toe-grip straw sandals used by judoka when in judogi moving to and from the mat edge.

Index